How Can We Be Wrong?
Max Austin

Copyright © by Max Austin.

Artwork: Adobe Stock – © thekopmylife, oasisamuel, pickup.

Cover designed by Spectrum Books.

All rights reserved.

ISBN: 978-1-915905-55-0

No part of this book may be used or reproduced in any manner whatsoever without written permission of the author of Spectrum Books, except for brief quotations used for promotion or in reviews. This book is a work of fiction. Names, characters, places and events are fictitious.

First edition, Spectrum Books, 2024

Discover more LGBTQ+ books at www.spectrum-books.com

Contents

Chapter One	1
Chapter Two	9
Chapter Three	20
Chapter Four	35
Chapter Five	47
Chapter Six	67
Chapter Seven	74
Chapter Eight	84
Chapter Nine	88
Chapter Ten	93
Chapter Eleven	98
Chapter Twelve	113
Chapter Thirteen	119
Chapter Fourteen	124
Chapter Fifteen	132
Chapter Sixteen	146
Chapter Seventeen	166
Chapter Eighteen	176

Chapter Nineteen	182
Chapter Twenty	191
Chapter Twenty-One	196
Chapter Twenty-Two	201
Chapter Twenty-Three	215
Chapter Twenty-Four	224

Chapter One

The clatter of the automatic doors closed tightly behind me as I left with my head full to the brim and already late home. My navy blue tunic had irritated fresh sunburn all day long. The first days back after a summer break are always a baptism of fire at the best of times, with or without ten hours of friction burns. Walking up to the staff car park after work was much harder than on the way into the hospital. I brushed past fresh lavender and my chest wheezed in disgust. Covid may have had its way with my lungs, but at least I was still here to tell the tale. Things could have been much worse. And indeed it had been for many NHS and social care staff up and down the country.

I took a second to catch my thoughts, switched on the radio, and turned the engine over. Thank goodness for air conditioning. I could finally breathe. That bathmat of a uniform was slowly relinquishing its grip on my sore bits. Adele's *Make You Feel My Love* soothed my soul as she sang out from the surround sound. Wayne was used to my lateness. It came with the territory of working as a nurse. As I turned left out of the hospital carpark, I noticed that some temporary traffic lights had been erected within the last ten hours and were now causing general pandemonium. Ambulances wailed on their way through the congestion and cars beeped each other in frustration. This unexpected pleasure was the last thing that I wanted. Right, that was it. I would find another way home if it killed me. Doubling backwards, I found another route. Having been born and bred around the hospital had its advantages. I knew all of the back alleys and side streets, even if it meant going around the reeking to get home.

Soon I was on King Street, under the shade of leafy oak trees, on my way past the cemetery and council allotments on my right. On my left was the old City Infirmary. This building was waiting for demolishment since the whole hospital was now located, lock stock and smoking barrel on one gleaming modern site. I'm sure that Prince Charles would have described this modern addition as one of those 'carbuncles'. Yes, it may have been functional, but it simply had no soul. The architects must have taken inspiration from a child's first attempt at building a Lego house. The traffic was going nowhere, I was crawling along. I pushed voice control and called Wayne.

"Hi Babe, I'm sorry, I'm stuck in traffic, expect me when you see me and tell the kids not to worry, sorry."

"Don't worry, Max, just get home safely. The kids are fine. They have had their tea and are now pretending to be Captain America and Iron Man on the trampoline outside. Anything to tire them out."

"Ok babe, send them my love and I'll see you when I see you."

And with that, I hung up and got back to Adele, who was now singing *Chasing Pavements*. I couldn't sit in the traffic any longer. I pulled up under the shade and decided to get out. It was amazing how nature takes over so quickly. Towers of buddleia had already broken through the abandoned staff carpark at the front of the hospital's former main entrance. And then curiosity killed the cat. I knew that it was wrong, but something was pulling me towards her. I wanted to see her and pay my respects to this Victorian lady for one last time. Before I knew what I was doing, I had sneaked through the debris and through her main door.

I could almost feel the weight of her sadness engulf me. A solitary tear drop from the leaking roof fell onto my head as I waded through her misery. Through her wounds, it was still possible to glimpse at the ornate beauty of her former life. Her peeling skin of cream emulsion flaked away in places to reveal the remnants of her previous grandeur. Above her old ward doors, it was still possible to see the names of pottery owners etched into the ornate tiles. These local businessmen were the original benefactors who gave birth to her long before the National Health Service had been conceived. She had carefully held the hand of both patients and staff for over two hundred years. Now betrayed, my old friend stood quaking in the fear of the imminent bulldozers.

Yet she still provided some comfort as I headed to the 39 steps of the City Infirmary. Over a period of years, the hard flagstones were worn smooth by a flurry of activity. Now caked in concrete dust, it was hard to imagine that these tombstones once provided the entrance to a secret world. In her heyday, they were affectionately called a 'stairway to paradise'. Many a courting suitor had fallen under their nocturnal spell in an attempt to enter the nurses' home. Their magic usually came to a swift end as a team of night sisters guarded the entrance to this medicinal fortress. Like St Peter at the gates of Heaven, their sole purpose in life was to protect the virtuous angels' reputation who lived in this ivory tower.

Filled with morbid unease, I navigated through the oak-panelled entrance of the nursing home half expecting to see the face of one of the old night sisters etched for prosperity within the wooden detail. Some ground-floor rooms had been converted into the 'staff support centre' and were festooned with poorly laminated signs of 'Quiet please'. The juxtaposition of providing such a haven for the well-being of staff in such a forbidding environment brought a wry smile to my face. It was like building a funeral home in Disney Land; it just didn't work. I wondered if the ghosts of the night sisters were present during the counselling sessions at the staff support centre, offering supernatural guidance from beyond the grave.

Amid this darkness, an alchemy of the past surged through my airway. My nose hair danced in delight due to the combination of hospital detergent and industrial polish. The familiar smell took me back to the roots of my NHS career in 1987 when I was employed as a Domestic Assistant. I was living at home with my parents and younger sister. My Dad, Oggy, worked in heavy industry and proudly described himself as a product of growing up in the sixties. He loved the simple pleasures in life; his family, going to the pub on a Friday night and his garden. Although money was tight, we were rich in love and happiness. My mother, Karen, saw to this. She walked with cardboard in her shoes to make ends meet. My mother got me the job as she worked as a Domestic Assistant herself.

Nick-named the 'majestic domestics' by the hospital staff, it appeared that working within the NHS was to become a family affair. Aunt Bren, my mother's sister, was also working as part of our domestic tribe at the Infirmary. Having been into 'wife swapping' parties in the seventies, Aunt Bren was now an extremely popular commodity at the Porter's lodge. She jangled her orchestra of costume jewellery, whilst almost suffocating her prey in cheap Avon perfume. It was no secret that she changed her men as often as her hair colour. Many of her gentleman 'friends' were enthralled by the charms of her intoxicating smile, candyfloss perm, low-cut cleavage and her passion for life. If nothing else, Aunt Bren was a survivor. Cackling playfully in an attempt to divert my anxieties, she said,

"As you have no doubt heard from your mother, Max, I have had more men than there are named within the bible. This includes both the new and old testaments put together. Let me tell you, I have no problem getting a man, but keeping hold of one is the trickiest part. Those greasy buggers seem to slip through my fingers."

I could feel myself blushing as I replied,

"Well, er, as long as you are happy."

And with this, my career working in the NHS began as we crossed the threshold to the Domestic Supervisors Office to clock on.

I had reached the heady heights of a 'floater'. My whole purpose in life was to relieve other domestics in times of holiday, sickness, and days off. This orange-clad army took good old-fashioned pride in their work. They were the Infirmaries' unseen hosiery that supported her Victorian splendour. And now, I was trying to hold up her knicker elastic, too. Many of the domestic staff had worked within the same area for years. I soon learned to be competent in taming the nemesis of the rotary floor cleaner. This beast commanded respect as we waxed and waned through the gleaming infirmary corridors together. It only took a moment of lost concentration to allow the power of this caged animal to release its anger into the world. With one prime evil scream, it would lunge its terror onto any unsuspecting passer-by. Such unforgiving wrath was in stark contrast to the delicate coordinated waltz with the 'kex' mop. This gentle lady shimmied in elegant adoration across any hard floor, almost grateful for the pleasure of the waltz. However, my right-hand weapons were a blue roll of industrial paper and a strong washing-up liquid called 'hospec'. With such strong allies at my side, we marched into battle at a moment's notice, tackling any unforeseen enemy together.

A regular battlefield became the accident and emergency department plaster room. The enemy was not the white dust that invaded every crevice, but the unmistakable temperament of Sister Jones. It was hard to see where the stark white tiled plaster room ended and she began. Every crevice of her wrinkled face was dusted in this white hue. It was like watching Bela Lugosi's Dracula. Armed with a scraper, I entered her crypt and began removing the debris of welded plaster. A young wet behind-the-ear cleaner was easy prey for anyone with an axe to grind. Sister Jones did not just have an axe, but a whole array of sagittal saws to play with. But she did have a reflection, after all. It loomed behind me in the stainless steel sinks as I worked. I could almost feel her eyes boring into the back of my neck as I did my best to stay upright. This unspoken persecution went on for months, as I was regularly called to her disposal. I tried to remain in her peripheral vision at all times until one day she reluctantly acknowledged my existence by gesturing a curt 'hello'. With dumbfounded confusion, I registered a stuttered 'h-hi' back to her.

This simple gesture signified the thaw of Sister Jones. In the new few weeks that followed, her stony mask began to crack like the patients' bones that she carefully wrapped in plaster of Paris. She only became alive when she gestured towards Charlie, a medical skeleton who was named after her husband. Sister Jones and Charles had a short and painful marriage together. She had walked away from the marital home clutching only her clothes. Over time, I began to receive small gifts from her as my lessons continued. On her way to her quarters at the Nurses Home, she often called into the staff canteen to buy me a piece of fruit or a chocolate bar. Even my mother was surprised by her kind gesture. For some reason that was best known to herself, Sister Jones had taken pity on me.

My mother raced through the hospital like Mary Poppins on amphetamines. Fuelled with the smell of stale coffee on her breath, she generated a physical warmth as she hurtled towards you. Dad affectionately called her the 'road runner'. On occasions, I had the pleasure of following her onto the same ward in the evening. She attacked the bathrooms with effervescent denture tablets in her quest to make enamel gleam. It was these little things that mattered to my mum. She even used an old knife and a Hoover tube to suck debris from in between the polished floorboards. It was mid-July, and I was getting hotter by the minute. A poor excuse of a floor fan hummed in the background as I served tea to the wilted patients of ward four. One of the student nurses jabbed me in the arm and told me that Mrs M was on the blower. She summoned me to the main entrance. In some strange kind of respect, domestic supervisors were referred to by the first letter of their surname.

The main entrance was a late seventies addition to the hospital, having the aesthetic appeal of an infected abscess. To the right of the main door was the obligatory shop, which sold curled-up sandwiches and an array of useless magazines. To the left was the registrar of deaths. I suppose that once registering the tragic loss of a loved one, it would be a natural occurrence to console your grief in the lives of some Z list celebrity or in a bag of out-of-date sweets. A prefabricated ramp then bounced the unsuspecting public to the main corridor of the hospital. On many occasions, I witnessed a wheelchair break free from its shackles and dive down the entrance ramp. Silhouettes of orange uniforms protected two women from the public gaze. Looking extremely composed amid this debris of torn stockings and unhinged perms, Mrs M made her single but direct request. She told me to take Aunt Bren home immediately before she was sacked on the spot. Fighting on the premises, especially in the public's eye, was tantamount to gross misconduct. Dishevelled but not defeated, I escorted Aunt Bren off the premises as she spat out to her opponent that 'no dirty cow messes with her family'.

Her adversary, Rita, made Lily Savage look like Mother Theresa. She had the grace and poise of a rhinoceros on heat. On turn-out day

I always got the short straw and reluctantly went to help her. Whilst generally causing pandemonium, a day was allocated to moving all of the patients and medical paraphernalia to one side of each ward to allow deep cleaning. Towering above her cleaning trolley, Rita wielded her high duster through the air with the precision of a sniper. I watched as she threw out hot drinks and sarcasm in endless supply. The split ends of her tightly pinned beehive were pebbled with the remnants of a cheap home highlighting kit. Ripples of fat seemed to move independently as she worked. It was quite ironic that Rita regarded herself as a lady's man since no man in his right mind would consider her to be anything of the sort. Unfortunately, the hospital grapevine was stronger than any drug or medicine. This invisible network of gossip raged faster than a case of diarrhoea and vomiting. Over a cigarette break, she bragged of her Saturday night secret sex against the urinals of the working man's club. She got her dabber wet while her husband and the man's wife played bingo. Bren hid behind the wheelchair store, stoking hate and venom in equal quantities until it was unleashed upon this foul-mouthed slut. She already knew that her father was a complete and utter bastard. But the rest of the hospital didn't need to hear this.

Chapter Two

But domestic life wasn't all hormones and heartache. As my confidence grew, Mrs M asked me to help Cynthia with the PM jobs. They had broken the mould when Cynthia was cast. Her pet name at the hospital was Joan Collins. But she didn't need to hide behind her crooked nylon wig that deliberately covered her hearing aids since she was as kind as she was glamorous. For years, she was given outside jobs, as her hearing loss made it difficult for her to communicate in the noise of a busy ward. These tasks included emptying the bins in the boiler room, cleaning the electricians' workroom, removing the rubbish (and page three pin-ups) that regularly accumulated within the porter's lodge, polishing various offices and buffing up the boardroom. Cynthia took great pride in servicing these unseen necessities of the busy hospital. As we cleaned and polished, she began to tell me snippets of her life. In a deep gravelly voice, she explained that although her sister had been killed in a car accident over thirty years ago, there wasn't a day that went by when she didn't miss her. Cynthia took in her daughter Pam and raised her as her own. Although now in her thirties, Pam still lived at home as 'she was unable to cope with the outside world'. Cynthia had never married, although she had been in a string of unsuccessful relationships. As she put it, 'no man would stick around long enough once they had met Pam'.

The 'pm' rota had nothing to do with completing afternoon jobs. No, it stood for post-mortem. The colour drained from me as Cynthia gripped my clammy hand. Where had all the air gone? Although this was the last job of the afternoon, it was my first experience of death. I could feel beads of cold sweat on my forehead and tasted a regurgitated bacon sandwich with each step closer to the mortuary. It was really strange that the staff social club was located next door to this art déco structure. In some parallel universe, it made perfect sense for the two buildings to be bedfellows. There would be no opportunity for complaints from the residents of the mortuary when rowdy staff left the social club. Well, I hoped not, anyway. I was naïve, but not stupid. I knew that patients died. However, this was the domain of the clinical team. My mother warned me to watch out for the empty porter's trolley that took the recently departed for their final journey. This metal coffin sang an unmistakable hymn of respect as it creaked through the Infirmary with a silent passenger hidden below.

Cynthia was still holding my hand as we crossed the threshold from the living to the dead. My first job was to empty bins full of God knows what. Metal lids echoed as I quickly replaced the yellow bags without looking. The laboratory was flooded with stained glass dappled light. A precession of dark oak work benches housed a collection of glass bottles and test tubes. Tubular taps gracefully glided like swan's necks towards blood-splattered enamelled sinks. The smell of caustic chemicals hit the back of my throat like cheap booze. Just as I was beginning to come to terms with my surroundings, Cynthia caught hold of my arm again. She beckoned towards shelves that seamlessly floated above the workbenches in the dark. Why was the floor suddenly spongy? A menagerie of pickled body parts floated towards me. A perfectly formed foetus in a large glass bottle looked out from its watery grave. A pickled head with piercing green eyes stared straight past me. A half-dissected hand gave me the birdie. If nothing else, I could take the hint and decided it was probably best to leave them to their own devices.

It was now time to clean the 'cut up room'. The same blue linoleum was used on both the sticky stairway of the staff canteen and the steps to the ground floor. However, food was the last thing on my mind. Cynthia's vain attempts to reassure me that the 'worst of it' had been removed did little to settle me. With each step down into the basement, I became increasingly uneasy as the stench of death grew stronger. A line of frothing white buckets seamlessly guided us into the mortuary changing room. Each bucket had a string tied to its handle. When a patient's brain was removed, it was suspended within the preserving solution. Like a jelly, it needed time to set before it could be sliced for further analysis. With a sigh of relief, I fell through the door and onto a hard wooden changing bench. With my head in my hands, I slowly registered a new voice. Someone or something was trying to talk to me.

A young wet stag appeared wrapped in only a white NHS towel. I didn't know where to look. He tried to shake my hand whilst keeping the towel around his waist,

"Oh, sorry, did I startle you? Usually, there is no one around at this time of the evening here. My name is Wayne."

"Hello, Wayne, no worries. My name is Max. I'm just trying to find my feet here, sorry."

"Yes, I can see. You look whiter than my patients. I take it that you are a mortuary virgin. Take it from me, it does get better."

Now fully dressed, he guided me to the protective clothing and continued with his banter. He said that he had originally applied to work in the catering department. As his qualifications were mostly science-based, fate led to a life of caring for the dead. He took two hearing aids from his locker, flicked back a mass of glossy brown hair, and delicately placed them in his lobes. He smirked and said that his patients never grew tired of his jokes. And then he vanished into the evening air.

Once changed, I joined Cynthia. She smiled and gently applied a drop of menthol under my nose. To my immediate relief, the cut-up room was light, bright and gleamed with respect to the recently deceased. All images of Frankenstein's laboratory were exorcised. This semi-circular theatre displayed three white enamelled slabs that could be viewed via a raised gallery. I was impressed that each slab had its own set of stainless steel instruments that were stored with care and attention. It was obvious that abundant amounts of respect and dignity were given to the deceased. Even the row of fridges that buzzed in the background was clean and ordered. All fear left me with every 'swoosh' of my blood-stained kex mop. Now and again, I caught Cynthia watching me from the corner of her eye. Even within this cold laboratory, her warmth touched me from the other side of the room.

The mortuary experience had stirred something unexplainably deep inside of me that I was not ready to acknowledge. According to Cynthia, I had passed some strange 'rite of passage'. I wanted to make a difference in the world before my brain ended up in a white frothing bucket, too. The lifeblood of the City Infirmary began to transfuse through my veins. Mrs M recognised my passion for the hospital way before I did. She now instructed me to work under my own steam. I enjoyed talking to the patients as I served hot drinks and collected their empty food trays. Many nurses rushed into the kitchen for a quick cuppa and gossip. Being a familiar face on the wards had its advantages. Junior staff divulged all of the latest scandals. My eyes were like saucers as a student nurse slurped out that a senior sister had been caught with her knickers around her ankles, entertaining an A and E doctor in the linen cupboard. He was married and she should have known better. The shame of it.

The sanctuary of the kitchen was always a welcome relief after sidling past Sister Dickson. She had ruled the roost in the male surgical ward for more years than she cared to remember. Rumour had it that the great love of her life had been killed in a motorbike accident. But she was just a mere slip of a girl back then. She had met her fiancé at one of the closely guarded hospital dances. Police cadets were cordially invited for an evening of polite conversation with student nurses. This supervised dancing went on under the chaperone of the night sisters' beady eyes.

Emily Dickson spotted him standing in the corner of the room. He looked so handsome in his black uniform. Through the crepe paper streamers, their eyes met, and then she quickly looked away again. Glistening fragments of light danced around the walls as the dulcet tones of Perry Como's *Magic Moments* drifted from a clapped-out gramophone. It was all excess within control. The starched seams of her emerald satin dress seemed to tighten as she made a beeline for the buffet table, grabbing a paper plate of dry cheese and pickle sandwiches. And then she sat with the other wall flowers in anticipation for the evening to start.

Emily was catapulted from her mother's apron strings and into hospital life. Her uniform provided the perfect disguise for her ignorance of the opposite sex. Whilst smiling sweetly and hoping no one would notice, she tried to re-adjust her bodice, which was now becoming uncomfortable. Unfortunately, she didn't notice a gentleman suitor approach her. The tall blonde man was now standing in front of her in bemusement. Clearing his throat, he said,

"I hear that these party frocks can be most uncomfortable if not whisked around the dance floor at least five times an evening. Would you care to dance?".

Startled into submission, Emily and her dress gracefully accepted his invitation. Before she knew what she was doing, she was in the arms of Ron. And there she remained for the next two years as they planned their future. They talked of watching their grandchildren play in the park as they walked hand in hand together through the hospital grounds. He bounced with boyish energy and optimism, always making her laugh at his terrible jokes. Although never daring to admit it, Emily was in love. However, Ron never quite outwitted the night sisters. Like Romeo, he even climbed three storeys of stairs to have his ardour dashed at the last minute.

Blurry-eyed and bewildered, Emily dutifully climbed the thirty-nine steps towards the night sister's office. What could Sister Murray want with her at three o'clock in the morning, and more to the point, why had she been called away from the male surgical ward? Trying not to touch the freshly varnished oak panels, she wondered what she could have possibly done wrong. Sister Murray was waiting for her at the end of the dark corridor. She peered from over her round spectacles which extenuated her plump features. It had been years since she had been let loose on a ward. She wouldn't have had the stamina to keep up with the clinical demands now. There were no words to do justice to the pain that Emily felt. Every fibre of her heart had been ripped out. It would have been kinder for her to die in the car crash than to live her life without Ron.

Sister Dickson lived and breathed her role. Her ivory hair was always immaculately pinned into place under a frilly white cap. Her starched navy uniform complemented the white arm ruffles. She instilled the virtues of her experience into junior team members,

"Now, nurse, you only have one chance to make the right first impression. You must always treat patients with the utmost respect and dignity in every situation".

Everything needed to be at a right angle to each other in her ward, including the patients. She tidied up the lockers, ensuring that the bedside tables were positioned with perfectly perpendicular precision. Playing a strange game of cat and mouse, she followed me from bed to bed. I had heard that she would even strip freshly made beds if the sheets were not in alignment. The other nurses on the ward simply smiled and continued with the daily routine of running the ward around her.

The jewel in the Infirmary's crown was her breathtaking former main entrance. Meticulously clad oak panels with engraved brass-handled doors lined the entrance. Once through, she dazzled her admiring visitors with six chandeliers that effortlessly gleamed like new stars. These beauties cast sequined sophistication over a black-and-white tiled entrance square. This cavernous space was like a luxurious ballroom. I imagined ladies in their finest silk, perched expectantly on the wooden benches that lined the entrance square, coyly waiting for their dance cards to be filled. Plumes of ceramic flowers were set into three arches across the entrance. The Victorians certainly knew how to turn utilitarianism into sumptuousness. I detected her delicate scent of furniture wax and hospec whilst marvelling upon a central staircase.

These sweeping stairs guided me to the hospital boardroom. There was a huge double oak door which seemed to signify the importance of all who entered this domain. Hung upon the dark oak panelling were enormous stately portraits of the Infirmary's original wealthy benefactors. As I carefully high-dusted this room, the pottery owners still stared down as if to pass judgement on the decisions made from the coffin-shaped boardroom table. You could still feel their power in the air. I carefully cleaned at least sixteen red cracked leather chairs which were imprinted with the bum cheeks of sizable decision makers. All I had to do was to surf my slender frame across the table to clean a square of dust that was annoying me. No one would see me if I was quick. Oh my God, what was that? An icy hand rested on the small of my back. I didn't dare to move. My breath was leaving stain marks on the mahogany. Eventually, I moved my head and slowly peered behind me. This intrusion came in the form of a sun-tanned man in his mid-thirties. Sliding back onto my feet, knocking his hand from me and dropping my duster, I babbled,

"Oh-h, I'm sorry you scared me. I thought you were a ghost. I didn't know that you were there, sir. You are so quiet. I was just trying to reach the centre of the table."

"I have not seen you here before. What a pleasant diversion," he boasted from his yellow teeth and thin moustache. "Oddly, you have escaped my attention. How long have you worked here?"

Tasting his stale breath on my lips, I ranted on, "For nearly twelve months, sir, I enjoy being part of the hospital. It is a lovely place to work, and I love spending time talking to the patients. This is my first time in the boardroom."

"So I see," he said whilst gently swaying his head slowly from side to side. "I have been watching you work for a while. I am impressed by your attention to detail. It is a long time since our table has shone like this. You would make a fine French polisher."

It was time for me to go. I gently backed away from his tight-knit, dusty blonde hair. It was only once through the boardroom doors that I felt safe. God knows what he wanted from me. For there was one thing that working as a domestic assistant had taught me; everyone in the infirmary had a place and woe betide you if you overstepped the mark.

One of my regular haunts was cleaning the accident and emergency department. The staff smoking room was positioned at the back of the unit. A brown-haired nurse with a shaggy pinned-up perm introduced herself from behind a plume of smoke as I emptied the bulging ashtrays.

"Do you want a fag, duck? You are welcome to join me. Sit down for a minute and take the weight off those brogues. I am Carla, and you are?"

"Max, thanks for the offer, but I don't smoke."

Carla was very easy to chat too, and I instantly clicked with her. During her breaks, she chain-smoked at least five cigarettes. She told me that her 'disgusting habit', as she put it, helped her to deal with the stress of working within the department. Her robust frame would not have looked out of place on a girl's rugby team. This made her perfect for dealing with the drunks who turned up on the weekend. I laughed when she said that she was waiting for a boob job on the NHS. Joking, she said,

"No love, I can tell what you are thinking. I want a breast reduction, not an enlargement. These jugs are killing my back and getting in the way of my ability to do my job. Not that the male patients complain, though. My boyfriend says that more than a handful is too much for any man. Every time I take my bra off, he nearly has a bloody heart attack."

Although only in her twenties, Carla's shining compassion was inspirational. This cherry lipstick diva may have only been four and a half feet in height, but she shone like an unsuspecting angel amid the chaos. I was in awe of her determination and passion. Occasionally, she would catch my eye and throw a smile at me as I cleaned. Something was changing in me. I began to feel as if I was always the bridesmaid and never the bride.

"Well, you need to do something about it and stop moaning if that is how you feel," Carla bluntly said over her third cigarette. "Now listen Max, we only have one chance at this life that we know about, so go out there and bloody live it, for God's sake!!".

She was right. She then casually dropped the bombshell that the City Infirmary was recruiting Health Care Assistants. This was the brainchild of the newly appointed director of nursing. Although in its infancy, the Health Care Assistant role was essentially developed to provide direct patient care and support to the nursing team. That was it. I was going to apply. I trundled down to the Nursing Directorate Office. Greeted with the warmth and charm of indifference, Miss Jenkson stared over her half glasses at my request for an application form. She had seen it all before and was crossing off the days in her mind until she retired from her role as secretary to the newly appointed and, in her opinion, over-inflated director of nursing. She wore her tweed twin set and pearls as battle armour against the changes that she had witnessed over the recent years. She longed for the 'good old days' when Matron and the night sister's word was gospel. She had no idea how this man had risen to the top of the nursing food chain so quickly. Slowly prising the application form from her perfectly manicured nails felt like gold dust. I sat with Carla as she painstakingly helped me complete it. And to my utter amazement, I was asked to an interview and even landed the job. They must have been desperate. What had I done now?

Chapter Three

I stood at the sewing room door clutching the chitty like a winning lottery ticket. Both the sewing room and the domestic supervisors' pigeonhole shared a dimly lit corridor. Mrs M winked when Maggie called me into the den of singer sewing machines that ranted in the background. With the demise of the local mills, she was catapulted from the cotton reels and into the Infirmary. Her worn fingers quickly had the measure of me. From the back of the store cupboard, she shouted,

"You are in luck Max, we have 32-inch waist trousers in stock and 40-inch tunic tops. Are you 31-inch leg?"

"Yes, that's right," I mouthed back, hoping that I had got the gist.

"I have also found some lilac epilates, too."

And then she passed me the keys to the castle. Erasure's *hideaway* provided the perfect backdrop as I rehearsed walking onto a ward in my bedroom mirror. Starched white cotton felt reassuringly comfortable against my bare chest. Now it was time for the perfect hairstyle. Gone was the boring side parting and in was a stiff quiff. A stainless steel fob watch hung on my breast pocket like the Tin Man's heart. When I thought about Carla, I began to well up again,

"Well, I can't send you out to a ward half-cocked, can I? I won't have you showing me up on your first day. Pin the watch on with pride. Come here and hug me, you daft thing, Max."

Grappling with her bosom, I dived in, trying to get my arms around her. She smelled of smoke and sweat after a twelve-hour shift, but I didn't care. Now within whispering distance of her foundation, I said,

"Thank you so much. You will never know just how much this means to me. You are one in a million."

And she certainly was, even if she did laugh and tell me to let go of her before her boyfriend saw us.

Next time, I'd break my shoes in before wearing them. This black leather was playing havoc with my heels. Luckily, a frenzy of lilac diverted my limp into boot camp. My eyes uncomfortably landed upon Claire, an old school friend who sized me up and then spoke from beneath her lilac Alice band.

"Hello Stranger, haven't you changed for the better? Where did that chubby lad go, Max?" she asked.

"I guess that you haven't heard the story of the ugly duckling, then?"

This was not the time and place for a reunion. High school was just horrible anyway and made worse because I wouldn't join in the regular grope behind the gym with the other teenage boys and girls. All walks of life sat on hard plastic chairs and one by one introduced themselves. A middle-aged woman had decided that a life on the pot banks was no longer for her. There were a few college leavers, and then there was me.

Danni, our trainer for the two-week induction period, introduced herself. Her blouse wafted in a kaleidoscope of chiffon vibrancy as she spoke. A doll-like face was complemented by round, red-rimmed glasses, short blonde spiky hair, and large parrot earrings that flew below her earlobes, manically punctuating her every syllable. Just as she was telling us to strap ourselves into the ride of our lives, the clatter of a late arrival fell through the door. Like a court jester, the man faked a dramatic apology to the group. His sturdy frame slumped into a chair next to me, brushing his hairy arm against mine as he fell backwards. It looked as if he was trying to squeeze himself onto one of those miniature chairs that you find in a school reception class. An exclamation mark of a blonde spiked quiff rested upon his short-brown hair. Jack knew how to work a crowd. They were like putty in his hand after his comic entrance. Even Danni was susceptible to his charm. With a hint of annoyance in her voice, she said to him,

"Well, trust you to be late. We have just finished introducing ourselves. Now it's time for your five minutes of fame in the spotlight, not that you need it," Mimicking Cilla Black in an episode of Blind Date, her face softened as she said, "What's your name and where do you come from, Chuck?"

"Sorry I'm late everybody. I went to the wrong place and got completely lost, which is ironic as I have just come out of the RAF. Luckily for Queen and country, I didn't fly planes, though. You can imagine the mess the country would have been in with me in a pilot's seat. I was gainfully employed as a chef and called upon to cater for our fabulous royal family on occasion. Well, the stories I could tell you, they would make your toes curl. I would have to shoot you all if I did, so I'd better keep my mouth tightly shut. Oh, my name is Jack by the way and I live with my partner Paul who is a Staff Nurse here at the Infirmary and...,"

"Well, Jack, 'by the way'", Danni interrupted, "it is good to have you finally here. I'm just pleased that you have signed the official secrets act as we haven't got any more time for your stories, I'm afraid. Now, let's get down to business."

Through the structure of the National Vocational Care Awards (NVQ), we would gain a documented assessment of our competence by linking theory to practice. I was blown away that the government had put so much thought into reshaping the provision of nursing care. Just like watching a George and Mildred sketch, I imagined Mrs Thatcher propping herself up against a pink draylon headboard in the middle of the night whilst scribbling down her plans. A gentle jab would stop Denis from snoring. After all, this lady was 'not for turning', even if it was three o'clock in the morning. Without taking a breath Danni said that we were going to be taught to wash and dress a patient, how to make a bed, how to apply correct manual handling techniques, how to feed a patient, how to document our findings, how to recognise different styles of communication methods, how to enter data onto the newly developed computer system, how to order ward stock, how to record blood pressure, temperature and pulse and how to recognise the deteriorating patient. And the list just went on. I was exhausted just watching her.

I tried to digest all of this new information over lunch. The staff canteen was located in the bowels of the Infirmary that was accessed from behind a large and heavy grey sliding door. Although management decisions were made at the boardroom table, it was the kitchen that fuelled this hospital. It was as if I was standing on the seafront in Blackpool as we got closer to the battered delights of 'fish day' Friday. Danni plonked herself at our scratched Formica table and announced,

"Let me tell you, the sister's lounge is very over-rated and the company can leave you wishing for more than just a drop of milk in your tea. Shove up and make room for me here, will you?"

In the corner of my eye, I could see Sister Dickson throw daggers at her as she chatted with the riff-raff. It was this very hierarchy that comforted Emily Dickson. How could some young upstart challenge the status quo? Who did she think she was?

"Is it true what Paul has told me about you, Jack?" Danni smirked as she gestured provocatively towards her salami roll, "It has come to my attention that you have a particularly well-suited nickname."

Spluttering his coffee, Jack replied, "What has my man been telling you now? Is there nothing sacred?"

"Paul told me that he calls you 'Miss Australia' because you are big down under," she announced at the top of her voice to all and sundry.

An uproar of infectious laughter shook our table as Jack graduated through fifty shades of red. And then it was my turn to become the butt of her jokes. But there was no material to work with. I hadn't rubbed shoulders with royalty or had a dynamic nursing career. I was just plain old Max with a new hairdo. Danni asked if I had any 'love interests' as she put it. And the answer was a firm 'no'. My first and last college girlfriend hung on my arm like a trophy bride. Girls were beautiful, but it never led to anything serious.

"Don't you worry about a thing. It doesn't matter where you have come from, it only really matters where you are going. Stick with us. We'll soon corrupt you," Danni said.

She made the training ward come alive by channelling Florence Nightingale herself. And then came bed bath day. Danni asked us to change into our swimwear to practice washing each other. Such experiential learning was designed to give a taste of the world seen through the patient's eyes. I had never experienced an enema either, but that argument just did not wash. I had to do it and that was that. There was a sudden swish from behind the cubicle curtain. Jack nearly knocked me over, catapulting me upon the hospital bed. He shrieked in a Southern American accent

"Tonight Dan-ni, I'll be sangin *Shtand by yo-ur Bed* by the one and only Miss Tammy Wynette."

He was laughing and singing like a hyena with a bad case of wind. Danni's annoyance just stoked his fire even further. He lay star-shaped on his back, waving his hands and feet in tandem to his poor rendition of 'Stand by your man'. The room collapsed into laughter. That would teach her for telling everyone his nickname, even if it was accurate. After taking communal showers for as long as he did, this was a walk in the park. I was relieved to be paired with him for our defrocking. Better Jack than the perfectly accessorised Claire. He was able to go from camp to calm in a split second. I just couldn't make eye contact as I gently washed his downy contours in the strict sequence that was required to complete the assessment. I carefully anointed his firm ripples with suds before drying him down with a rough NHS towel. Finally, my fingertips left him. Our eyes locked for a second, and then he said,

"You did well. Don't worry Max, there is a first time for everything, isn't there?"

And with that, it was my turn to be the patient. I stripped off to reveal a pair of crimson boxer trunks that matched my blotchy rash. Unfortunately, histamine does not lie. Jack washed my lank figure with skill and ease. Breaking my silence, he said,

"You will be fine with me. Just try and relax; we are not going to play 'let's hide the soap' today. Anyway, it's a good job that we are not using Lynx body wash. This will go down in the bed bath hall of fame when I am finished with you."

"You're not exactly helping here, Jack."

I lay rigid on the starched hospital sheet. He talked me through the process as I counted the ceiling tiles, biting my lip until his hands were done. And then I breathed. I caught a glimpse of him in the mirror whilst changing. He was silent but simply put his hand on my shoulder.

Where had the time gone? Our two-week induction period had flown past. Jack invited me to his home to celebrate our survival. Jack and Paul lived in a terraced cottage, located only a few streets away from the Infirmary. As he said, their home was close enough to fall out of bed and be at work in five minutes, but far enough away to escape the hospital grapevine. I gratefully accepted the invitation and then spent the next two hours stressing about what to wear. After much deliberation, I decided on a pair of tight white jeans, a pale blue denim shirt and my black leather biker's jacket. Armed with an alcoholic Blue Nun under my arm, I skipped from my parent's house, into town and through to the outskirts of the Infirmary before finally arriving. A rustle of activity rang from behind a crimson crushed velvet curtain. Jack answered the door and beckoned me into their reception room.

It was dimly lit with multi-coloured Christmas tree lights that hung happily around a black wrought iron fireplace. I studied the collection of photographs displayed on the mantelpiece. Jack peered proudly from a gilded frame, looking handsome in his RAF uniform. In total contrast, a picture of Jack and Paul in full Rocky Horror Show splendour took centre stage. Since the show had started locally, they felt duty-bound to honour its tradition. Jack explained that it was almost impossible to walk in size thirteen stilettos. He came close to splitting his difference. Those fishnets chaffed terribly in the crotch as the pair tittered through the city centre together. My eyes rested on a picture of Danni and Paul. They had trained together as nurses and had remained as close friends ever since. Donned in full cap and gowns, they proudly waved their certificates like two young surfers. If anything, this friendship backfired during the training weeks. As he explained,

"It did me no favours. How can I compete with Paul? He is such a hard act to follow. Oh, by the way, I forgot to mention that the woman in question and her awful earrings are coming over too. I hope that is ok?"

Paul appeared from the kitchen, smiling, and said,

"What is going on in here? I can hear so much laughter. You must be Max. I have heard so much about you. Please kick off your shoes and make yourself at home."

And with that, I saw the back of his blonde curly locks disappear as a wave of home-cooked delights wafted from the kitchen door.

Scented candles danced provocatively across the ruby walls. The aroma of bergamot and lavender soothed me. I sat cocooned in a brown leather Chesterfield covered in fluffy tartan blankets. A series of welcoming bean bags dotted the stripped floorboards. Paul re-appeared, offering me a warm drink and a chocolate biscuit. He was the yin to Jack's yang. I could see why he was good at his job. I imagined him comforting distressed patients, projecting calmness from his curly halo. Now into his early thirties, this barefoot man was dressed in a linen shirt and a pair of faded jeans. His glorious locks were tied back with a white headband, exposing soft facial features. To be honest, he wouldn't have looked out of place etched into a stained-glass window. Although the couple sat opposite each other, I could feel the passion burning between them. And for the first time in my life, I was jealous and wanted someone to feel that way about me.

Peering at me through the candlelight, Jack told me the real reason for this invitation. The long and short of it was for some reason, he didn't want anything bad to happen to me. Taking a slurp from his tea, he explained,

"The only dishonourable discharge I had before leaving the RAF was when I was stationed in Cyprus, and that was soon cleared up with a course of antibiotics. I don't want anyone to go through anything like that. My parents are ashamed of me. They are still not talking to me now."

I had been breathing through a straw for too long. It was no good. I couldn't hold it in for one moment longer. And in that incense-infused, fairy-lit moment, it was time to release the beast in safety. With the poise and drama of a nineteen-thirties Hollywood actress, I blurted out,

"I am suffocating. Please help me. I can't make sense of my head. I think I am gay. No, I don't think, I am gay, but don't know what to do about it. You have got closer to me over the last two weeks than anyone else ever has."

And there it was. I had done it. My truth was finally out.

"Well, enough of the drama Max, tell me something that I don't know. We are not in an episode of EastEnders, you know. Personally, I blame the bed bath. It's all Danni's fault. You will be ok, we will look after you."

When the city infirmary extended her delicate hands, I never thought that she would provide me with a family, too. Danni then appeared in the middle of the floor show, looking puzzled in an even bigger pair of glasses. They gave her a Deidre-esk vibe from 'Coronation Street'. Whilst badly mimicking Cilla Black again, she quipped,

"Have I stepped into the right house, Chuck? I thought I had walked into an episode of Surprise Surprise."

Jack's eyes twinkled as he said, "For the love of Christ, please don't sing Danni. We have had enough drama to last us a lifetime tonight."

And with that, the rest of my life changed, finally my heart was connected to my head. But Danni had news of her own, too. Over tea, she told me I was on my way to a male medical ward. Gulp.

I turned up for an early shift. With every step, my heart beat a little faster. Taking a final check in the windows, I pushed the ward door open and made my way to the staff room. I was met by a bunch of nurses who were sucking the last drag from a fag before reporting for duty.

"Hi Max, welcome to paradise," a sultry voice announced from over the commotion.

As the smoke dispersed, I spotted Vivien, the junior ward sister. She was a slender vixen in her late thirties and would not have looked out of place in the hunting set. I watched her tie her jet-black hair into a ponytail and then top up her lipstick. She then adjusted her navy uniform to ensure the ornate silver buckle was displayed in full star-spangled pride of place.

Springing to her feet, she said, "Come on girls, let's get this show on the road. The night staff will be ready for their beds by now. Oh, sorry, can I introduce you to Max? He is our newest recruit."

Since many of the team already knew me, my introduction was less bumpy than I had expected. As I followed the team down a long corridor from the staff room to the nurses' station, I became acutely aware of the hierarchy. Vivien led the precession, followed closely by a couple of staff nurses, then two enrolled nurses and finally the troop was completed in the rear by two health care assistants. As we filed into the ward, Vivien glanced back and smiled at me. This medical ward had recently undergone a refit. Gone was the cavernous nightingale ward and in were four, six bedded patient bays that were conveniently positioned around a central nursing station. There were also a series of four side rooms jotted around the ward in-between state-of-the-art medical equipment and bathrooms. A familiar voice drifted towards me as I stood nervously around the nursing station, contemplating my fate.

"Well, you didn't think that you would escape me that easily, did you? Danni thought it would be a good idea following my breast surgery if I had a break from A and E for a while. I have been training as one of these new-fangled healthcare assistant assessors on the quiet.

I thought that you could be my first, so to speak," Carla announced from her new but more than adequate bosom.

I was like a dog with two dicks. Thank God she was here. As we stood around the nurses' station and received a handover from the night nurse in charge, patients' names, ages, medical histories and care needs were discussed with the vitality of the Swedish Chef. It just made no sense to me, and to make matters even worse, many of the words were abbreviated to save time. I had no idea what was meant by 'he has had a CVA, PE and DVT, he is on qds obs and a 1 in 8 IVI, we need SALT as he is NBM'. This Pentecostal Preacher was connecting to her congregation in divine tongues by the time her sermon had finished. Carla patted my hand, smiled, and then jumped into action. On our way to the bay of patients, she said,

"Right, listen to me and remember these words. In your nursing career, you will see all sorts of practice. However, I will show you how to do things properly. These will be the tools in your nursing bag. Never drop your standards. And while I am at it, remember they are people and not 'bed 22'. I hate it when I hear that phrase."

Out was the fag smoking crudeness and in was professionalism. We went from one patient to the next, introducing ourselves and reading the records at the end of their beds. Even the tone of her voice changed to quiet professionalism. I was in complete awe. We introduced ourselves to Sam. This man has been admitted to the ward due to unstable diabetes. He sank into the white cotton sheets as we chatted and gained his consent to help him wash. The reality of this bed bath was far different from the sterility of my healthcare school experience. There was a fine art of navigating through the spaghetti junction of drips and infusions. Behind the privacy curtains, he started to cry. He told us that life had lost its sweet taste since his Marg had died two years earlier. His eyes twinkled as he talked about her. She did not care for fancy holidays, expensive clothes or going out. His home bird had now flown the nest and had taken his heart with her. And then I saw the power of nursing. Carla said that whilst she understood how he felt, she was almost sure that Marg wouldn't like to see him neglecting himself. And that was all he needed right now, but been given far more than a bed bath. A strange thing was happening around me. Whilst on the ward, all the nurses were the definition of kindness. However, once in the staff room, they cackled and joked together like naughty schoolgirls. Vivien was intrigued by Carla's new physique. Sputters of giggles shook the staff room when I inadvertently arrived, just as Vivien had a handful of Carla's slim-line breasts. They were comparing notes.

Later in the day, the atmosphere changed from quiet compassion to a turbulent storm when Sister Lowly appeared. Her three-foot statue was exaggerated by a pork pie bonnet that precariously balanced upon her tightly pinned black hair. This bulldog's thick-rimmed glasses rested on rippled jowls. I thought I was going to wet myself. Before I could speak, Carla jumped in.

"Sister Lowly, let me introduce Max. As you have been informed, he is your new healthcare assistant. As you are already aware, I am here to support his learning."

She looked at Carla as if she had discovered a skid mark on a hotel towel. I watched her flare her nostrils before retaliating from beneath her frilly hat,

"I *was* aware, thank you, and it will do you good to remember whom you are talking to before you open your less-than-experienced mouth to me in that tone. You are only here because of him. This is my ward and always remember that, Carla. Max, I will see you in my office at three. I like to see all of my new starters in person."

Now I was in for it. At three o'clock, I was summoned into her slaughterhouse. The office was a wooden-panelled extravaganza of dusty fake flowers and medical books. In the centre of the dark room was a crusty brown swivel chair. Sister Lowly's ample frame was wedged into the seat like a human beanbag. Cold sweat dribbled down my spine as I sat down. Although only seconds, the silence was killing me. Passing me the handle to a bone china mug, she smiled, then said,

"How is your lovely Aunt Bren, Max? She is one of the best domestic assistants that has ever graced my ward. And so too is your mother. You have a very hard act to follow. I'm running a hospital ward and not a pub here so kindly address me as Sister at all times. But, if you work hard and keep to my rules, then you will do well."

Whilst nearly spitting my lukewarm tea at her, I replied,

"Yes, Sister. My Aunt Bren and Mother are fine, thank you for asking Sister," with as much sincerity as I could muster for her.

The creak of her door opening captured the attention of Vivien, who gave me one of those 'knowing' smiles. But Sister Lowly was right. With work, grit, determination, and a bit of luck, I did do well. I had no idea what I was capable of doing.

Joan taught me about death with her intoxicating zest for life. This butterfly had never married and had been happy to fly around the world as senior cabin crew. Winking at me through her concoction of chemotherapy, she explained,

"My darling, image is everything. Even when exhausted after a long haul to Tinsel Town, I had my standards. You see sweetie, glamour is fifty per cent illusion and fifty per cent extravagance." Stopping in mid-sentence to adjust her headscarf and cream silk Kimono, she continued, "I never knew whom I was going to meet. I mixed with high society from all over the world, darling Max. And what would they say if they saw me like this?"

I held her hand, being careful not to dislodge the needle, and replied, "It doesn't matter what they would say now, does it? The only thing that matters is what is important to you."

And then I saw her. She quietly whispered, "You will make sure that I look my best, won't you, Max?".

"Yes, it is the very least that I can do for you."

Joan loved opera. I asked her if it was the music itself that she liked so much, or had she just got a thing for men in tights? What was a codpiece amongst friends? A cassette of her favourite pieces drifted from her room, filling the ward with calmness. Maria Callas was playing as Joan shared her final moments with me. She took one last exhausted breath, smiled and closed her eyes. The grip on her hand became loose as we sat together, waiting for the music to end. I washed her, secured her headscarf, applied her favourite lipstick and carefully wrapped her into a hospital sheet before the porters lowered her into the metal mortuary trolley.

Life was like sitting on both ends of a seesaw at the same time. Work was tough, but I wanted a little fun too. Jack held my clammy hand as he launched me down the red-lit corridor, through a guarded door, and onto the gay scene for the first time. We were faced by a tall reptile dressed in a dandruff-covered doorman's uniform. Whilst undressing me with his eyes, through nicotine-stained teeth, he said,

"Well, well, well. Hello, my darlings, a virgin have we here? What's your name, my chicken? If you want to come in, then you will have to kiss me on my lips or anywhere else you fancy. I'm not fussy. I always get the first taste before anyone else, as Jack knows all too well." Whilst sliding his hand over Jack's thigh, he continued, "I remember everything, Jackie Boy. Awe, bless you, how you shivered outside my welcoming entrance in those tight shorts and ripped T-shirt. Come rain or shine, you never failed to turn up, did you now? Such dedication to the cause."

"Get lost Myrtle, take your grubby hand off my leg and leave us alone you filthy bitch," Jack spat back.

And with that, my journey into the gay scene began. And what a ride it was with more twists and turns than the coast road from Newquay to Padstow. I could give Aunt Bren a run for her money any day of the week.

Chapter Four

Jack almost spats his vodka and coke at me over the bar. What was he trying to say over the top of this vibrating pulse? I could feel him gyrate to the rhythm of *It's A Sin* by the Pet Shop Boys as he spoke,

"Can you hear me now? If I get any closer, Myrtle will be telling us to get a room. Will you just apply for your nurse training and stop feeling sorry for yourself? *When I look back upon my life, it's always with a sense of shame, I've always been the one to blame.* You are getting on my tits. For the love of Christ, change your record. *For everything I long to do, No matter when or where or who.* What is the worst thing that can happen? *Has one thing in common too, It's a, it's a, It's a, It's a sin.* After all, Max, there is nothing wrong with you. You are a very quick learner. I have seen that here over the last twelve months. So do me a bloody favour and make it happen before I pour my drink over you. *Everything I've ever done, Everything I ever do, Every place I've ever been, Everywhere I'm going to, It's a sin.* You don't need a fairy godmother and anyway, I have left my wand at home. You just need to believe in yourself for once."

He was right, even if he did camp it up to make me listen. There was nothing to lose. Well, accept my self-respect and dignity, that is. I enjoyed my job as a health care assistant but wanted bigger, better, and more. Much like my time on the gay scene in all honesty. Following the completion of a long application form and a gruelling interview, it was good news; I had done it. It was time to start my life as a student nurse. What had I done now?

Tapping my foot on the concrete steps, I waited for the doors to open. There were no night sisters but just the equally terrifying home warden, Mrs Greenstick. Somehow, I had landed a penthouse room. A Flamingo-themed message board looked proud as punch in the centre of my new red door. I walked over to the attic window and saw the mortuary and staff social club. I was home. Mrs Greenstick ranted rules and regulations at me before scuttling off.

There was a small sink, a built-in wardrobe, a fold-away desk, and a worn bed frame. The shower block and kitchen were positioned within spitting distance. Perfect. Silverfish slithered from out of the shadows and onto my bed. But nothing could put me off my piece of heaven in the sky. I took out a picture of my sister and unpacked my belongings. This wouldn't take long. Before I knew it, I was in the land of nod. God knows how long I had been out. Jumping up from my unmade bed, dusting off silverfish, I staggered towards the door. Still rubbing my eyes, a ginger mop of curls and freckles chirped,

"Hello roomy, I'm Tracey. I have just moved in across the hall. Are you starting your nurse training too? What's your name?"

"Max," I said whilst she stopped to take a breath through the crack in her front teeth. "But I'm sorry, we are not allowed to keep pets here," I added.

Tracey's face lit up. She waved her legs at me like a cancan dancer. "I will take it that you don't like Pinkie and Perky?"

"What! You have named those pig slippers?"

Then she whisked me across the landing and into her room without so much as a second thought for her safety. For all she knew, I could have been a serial killer, hell-bent on the mass genocide of student nurses. Her pad was a carbon copy of mine. Even the sink gurgled the same song. The main difference was our outlook, as she overlooked the busy medical block. The view of the mortuary was suddenly far more appealing than before. Hopefully, nobody could stare into my room. I thought about Wayne working hard beneath me. Whilst Tracey made a cuppa, I clocked her bedside shrine. A small wooden crucifix, turquoise rosary beads, and a picture of the Virgin Mary sat proudly between the livestock.

Her parents were big in the Southampton catholic community. After being roped into polishing the church, running Sunday school and attending the plethora of meetings, Tracey had little time for herself.

"So you have run away then? Was the thought of living under a cassock and wimple too much? It's not exactly like the Sound of Music, here either," I quipped.

She quietly replied, "How did you guess? Yes, that's right, I don't want to be a nun, what else could it be? Silly me. Well, if we are playing Mastermind, why have you moved into the nurses' home? I recognise your accent, Max. Only locals with mitigating circumstances are welcome here."

It was time for a taste of my own medicine. And who could blame her? It must have been the influence of her makeshift altar, but I decided to confess,

"Well, you see, my parents weren't exactly over the moon when they discovered that they had a 'fairy' for a son. Being closer to the infirmary is just easier for everyone. I didn't fancy my chances on the streets. I sofa-surfed for a while before I got my place in here."

By the fourth cup of tea and sympathy, we were firm friends.

Even the stench of stale smoke and urine-soaked seats could not dampen our excitement. Why do all buses smell the same? Only tube trains are worse. Tracey and I chatted like two fishwives as the double-decker chugged on. There was no room at the inn for eighty new student nurses at the hospital site. So we rode the five miles or so per day to our affiliated university. This was no hardship as the campus was stunning. A plethora of academic lecture theatres straddled a grand hall. All of the buildings sat in beautifully kept grounds and woodlands. Although the landed gentry was long gone, their legacy still resided over our learning. The ancestral hall stood proud and handsome as if to say 'Look, I'm here, admire me'. Although more used to wedding parties and the conference circuit crowd these days, it still commanded respect.

We followed the signs past the grand hall and into one of the cookie-cutter lecture halls, sitting next to a friendly-faced man in his late twenties. Turning to us, he said slowly in a thick Yorkshire accent,

"Hello, good to see you maties, my name is Kev. I see we are all in it together. Pull up a pew and make yourselves at home."

He was a quarter goth, a quarter rocker, a quarter bad boy and now a quarter student nurse, as he put it. It turned out that his room was only a few doors away from us at the nurses' home. As the performance began, all I needed was a bag of popcorn. The cast of smartly dressed men opened act one. The audience let out a shushed rumble as the first tutor spoke,

"Well, hello and welcome. My name is Sam McGreave. I am one of the senior lecturers here. Welcome to the first day of your three-year nurse training. As you are aware, you have enrolled to be our pilot of Project 2000. This is a new approach to training, where academic ability is placed as high as the practical skills of being a nurse. We are not training just any old nurses; no, we are training our leaders of the future," he enthused.

I expected this slender short haired man to burst into a verse of YMCA by the Village People or something as equally irritating. But to my relief, he continued with.

"During the first eighteen months of your nurse training, we place as much importance on homeostasis as we do on the study of illness. Within this common foundation programme, you will all study the same subjects. Then you will branch off into adult, mental health, or learning disability specialisms. At the end of your training, you will not only be registered as a newly qualified nurse, but you will also have a diploma to your name! This is a brand-new concept, so the going will get tough. Only the brave will survive. As I said earlier, you are our nurses of the future. A lot is resting on your shoulders."

I didn't know whether to be flattered by this man's incredible enthusiasm or to be insulted by his naivety. Suggesting that we were a new breed implied that what had gone before didn't matter anymore. The past couldn't be dismissed by the invention of Project 2000. Traditionally trained nurses had tended to the needs of the City Infirmary for many decades. They wouldn't just roll over to the latest whims in nurse training for man or beast. The likes of Sister Dickson, Sister Jones, or indeed Sister Lowly would not take this one lying down.

I threw myself into student nurse life at a rate of knots. Kev and Tracey regularly fought for a spot on my red bean bag as we passed the nights away to music, chat and occasional study. But it wasn't just my clinical confidence that was growing. There were more notches on my headboard than all of the bed frames at the Infirmary put together. Tracey and Kev got sick of hearing Enya or The Mission bellowing out in code to warn them away. I smuggled men in, right under Mrs Greenstick's nose, as she believed they were study buddies. Well, they were helping me to brush up on my anatomy and physiology. I knew that the men wouldn't love me tomorrow, but if I was honest, I didn't care.

All of this changed over lunch at the nurses' home canteen. Kev and I sat in our usual plastic chairs, picking our way through a cheese flan. The chairs were connected to the metal table frame. This had the effect of sitting on a trampoline whilst trying to eat. Any rash movement could bounce our food off the table. I found it difficult to hear Kev over the clatter of plates. What was he on about now? Yes, I finally got it. He was suggesting a sponsored bed push into the town, followed by a disco, to raise money for the air ambulance. And then we were abruptly interrupted.

I looked up to see a male nurse beaming down at us. Kev raised his eyebrows and smirked. Whilst gently kicking me under the table, he asked the man if he liked Enya.

Looking puzzled, he replied, "Yes, as a matter of fact, I do. Hi, is it Max? I have seen you at the club and I have been meaning to say 'Hello' for a long time, but my jealous ex would have none of that. Can I sit down?"

"Yes, I am Max. Yes, please join us. This annoying fool is named Kev. Take no notice of him."

"I know who you are, Max. I worked briefly with Jack last month. He is such a nice bloke. He thinks the world of you. Are you two an item? My name is Daniel."

What a small world the Infirmary had turned out to be. Everyone knew everyone else. I was becoming hot under the collar and stuttered,

"Good God, no. We are not like that. It would be like sleeping with your older brother."

"Well, that is good news for me then, isn't it?" he smirked.

With hook, line, and sinker, he carefully reeled me in. And I didn't even realise that he was doing it. Kev tapped me with his leg as if to say that it was rude to stare, but I couldn't help myself. He ran his hands through his curly black hair as we chatted and slowly inched his fingertips until we were touching. There was much more than the smell of cheese flan in the air. He had originally trained as a chef and only returned from the big smoke to start his nurse training. A small staff cottage on the outskirts of a semi-rural hospital was just a lovely place to grow up with his four brothers. We spent many a happy evening together staring into the open fire whilst his dad plied me with his latest home brew and his mum fed me fruit cake. Daniel was a country bumpkin at heart and no stranger to a roll in the hay, either. Nothing was finer than a good ramble through the long grass together. It was like being an extra from an episode of Darling Buds of May. In the words of that other drama queen, Madonna, I had definitely made it through the wilderness and into the third year of my nurse training. And more to boot, Daniel did make me feel shiny and new. What a trophy.

We lay panting together in the soft grass. Still coming down from euphoria, my hands gripped the fresh grass beneath us. Even the rain hadn't quenched our thirst for each other. We were splattered in each other's muddy handprints. But when the mood takes you, you have to do what you have to do. He leaned over me and rested on one elbow. Taking a handful of mud, he now began to draw love hearts on any patch of clean skin.

"Well, my dirty boy, I suppose this is as good of a time to tell you as any. I've got a new job. And you are not going to believe this one either. I'm going to train as the first male midwife in the area. Yes, me, can you believe it? Times are finally changing. I didn't want to say anything until I was sure."

In between slapping filthy kisses on his face, I said, "Oh, my God, that's amazing. I'm so proud of you. But what would people say if they could see you now, you horny bugger?"

And with that, we were off again. There was no better way to celebrate his hard work. Once scrubbed and cleaned, we headed to the City Infirmary. Much like our earlier ramble, the hospital propaganda machine was stoked, primed, and ready to explode. A couple of days later, the local rag sported the front-page headline of 'Daniel delivers more than just diversity'. And just like all good politicians do, a black-and-white photo of him holding a baby shone from the front page, in a similar ilk to those beautiful Athena posters. I often admired a framed window display of a doting muscular father holding the fragility of his newborn. And now I had my real-life poster boy to ogle at. It was just a pity that I couldn't have a child to complete our family. I would give my right arm for that chance, even if it was just fantasy. Jack well and truly put his size eleven feet in it when Daniel showed him the news story. I wanted the ground to open up and swallow him whole. On seeing the picture, he said that the Infirmary could have found a better-looking baby to pose with. He was oblivious that this was not just any random baby that had been plucked from the maternity ward. No, this was Daniel's nephew.

Our Victorian lady was beginning to loosen her tightly guarded corset. She stepped slowly towards her rainbow-filled future. However, not everyone was supportive of Daniel's new training. Sister Dickson dismissed the idea as ludicrous, saying that there 'was no place in nursing for men, let alone within midwifery'. Her sentiment echoed through the more traditional elements of the nursing ranks, ruffling those archaic feathers. However, I really couldn't give a monkey's chuff.

Like most things in life, my time at the nurses' home came with an expiry date. Uncertainty hung in the air like Aunt Bren's heavy perfume. Kev had already flown the nest and was living with his fiancé. Tracey planned to move into a shared rental near the hospital. Following a tip-off, I approached a local housing association that specialised in placing low-income earners. I was over the moon to find out that they had a one-bedroom flat with my name on it. Everyone has to start somewhere. And my start was slap bang in the middle of the red light district. It was a poorly carved mash-up from a much grander building. In its former and less salubrious life, this Victorian Villa probably housed a pottery manager and his family.

A communal hallway led the way to the flat, where an exotic aroma got stronger with every step up to the middle floor. All of a sudden I was pleasantly relaxed but unusually hungry. The door looked like it had been kicked in a few times. It rattled uncomfortably as I prized it open and stumbled into a dark entrance square. Immediately in front was a newly installed bathroom suite. To the left was a perfectly adequate double bedroom. This had a picturesque view of the bins, a carpark and some derelict terrace houses. One of the working girls had been recently murdered in the houses as she plied her trade. The front room was gigantic and sported a bay window with a view of the main road. From here you could see all the necessities of life, including a row of shops, a pub, an off-licence and even an army barracks. Off this main room, there was a small kitchenette. The flat was less of a do-er upper and more of a 'do-er downer'. Plaster fell off every wall and an unholy stench attacked my nostrils as I wandered through. It was as if something had curled up and died behind the hot water tank. And, in all honesty, it probably had.

I found a rickety old rocking chair in the living room. After checking for splinters and knowing that I was up to date with my tetanus jab, I risked it. Rocking and creaking, creaking and rocking over and over again, I weighed up my options. You didn't have to be Anna Ryder Richardson to see that the flat needed so much work. But it was going to take far more than two days, five hundred pounds and the skills of 'Handy Andy' to do anything with the state of this neglect. But this is all that I could afford. There were two clear choices. I could move in and make a go of it or find a room in a shared house. In a moment of madness, I'd decided. I was going to bring this flat kicking and screaming back to life. Daniel was nearly as excited as me when I got hold of the keys. Thankfully, he decided to move in and help out with the bills. Otherwise, I would need to implement my 'Plan B.' Well, I was living in exactly the right spot for a boy to earn a little money to make ends meet. Mrs 'M' 'donated' an assortment of cleaning products. She passed me the bucket full of goodies and offered to inspect my work, for old times' sake. Bless her, she had even decorated my gift with a couple of L plates. A card was wedged in between a packet of rubber gloves and a bottle of bleach. Money fell out onto her desk as I opened it. You see, once a domestic, always a domestic. Some moments are priceless, and this was one of them. Even Rita had donated to the collection.

"Now, listen to me, Daniel. You may be high and mighty at the hospital, but to me, you are just a scrubber under my control. Zip yourself into your moon suit and just get on with it. You can't have the gain without the pain. Are we clear?" I laughed but meant it.

"Yes sir, no sir, three bags full sir", he saluted before getting to work.

We scrubbed and polished every inch of our new home with military precision. Under my command, he did exactly as he was told. I was sure that there was a cure growing for some contagious disease at the bottom of the kitchen cupboards. It stunk far worse than anything

I had ever come across at the hospital. And that included the mortuary too. We found a few clues to the flat's illustrious past as we disinfected everything in sight. There were bullet holes in the bathroom walls. It took me ages to plug the random pattern with filler. The bathroom carpet was past repair. This beast reeked like one of Satan's farts as we lifted it. Thank God for face masks. The carpet hid the etched outline of a body upon the vinyl beneath it. It turned out that my bathroom was the scene of a violent crime. A drug lord was shot in the head here and then fell to his instant death. I imagined his blood-splattered head, breaking across my walls. We debated on whether to paint the outline of the figure with red paint. That would certainly provide a talking point over dinner parties. In the same ilk of why we should leave the Titanic well alone, it was finally covered.

You could set your watch by the paranormal activity in our flat. Precisely at the same time each night, a heavy clock on the fire hurtled at me. There were better ways to tell me that our ghost didn't like the freshly painted shade of the sea breeze. A very strange phenomenon happened on each side of the chimney breast. Two pictures magically moved around in their black frames. Maybe he wasn't a fan of Jack Vettriano either. Well, there is no accounting for taste. Guests would stare dumbfounded when all of this happened right in front of their very eyes. Jack found this parlour trick extremely fascinating until I told him about the shooting. Draining through fifty shades of green, he vowed that he would never use the bathroom again. He decided to find refuge in the army barracks across the road when the call of nature took him. Well, that was his excuse, anyway. To be honest, I think he wanted to play hide the soap again. Old habits die hard.

The living room carpet strangely showed no signs of wear and tear. As I crouched down, it stunk of a thousand fishy sins. I found out that it had been covered in a series of mattresses which protected it from foot traffic. My flat was a flop house. As the name suggests, punters flopped onto the communal mattresses and into a frenzy of public sex. This explained the bag of condom wrappers that I found shoved in the cutlery drawer. It took us over a week to completely clean the one-bedroom flat. It now smelt of bleach and hospec rather than the unsavoury reek of its former life. Old sheets were pinned up as makeshift curtains over the vast bay window.

Every night, whatever the weather, I left a flask of tea, coffee and a few snacks under the wheel arch of my car. It offered a little relief for the working boys and girls. In return, they watched over my car to ensure that all four wheels were still present each morning. The workers knew that I needed to get to the City Infirmary to care for the sick. This was better than any car alarm. We were all just trying to rub along together in whichever way we could. Quite often, I wandered across the pelican crossing like Noel Coward dressed in only a red silk dressing gown and a pair of slippers. It never occurred to me to do anything else. Someone was always on hand to serve me a bottle of knockoff booze, whatever the time of night. Within this flat, I had stumbled upon everything that I could need or want; love, safety, and community.

Chapter Five

I have been recently told by a senior manager that the condition for effective leadership relies on one main thing. Apparently, an NHS leader needs to move on from what clouds their judgement by leaving themselves at the door when they enter work. But this manager is wrong. We are not drones or numbers on a payroll. We are people with life experiences that should make us more aware of the needs of others. I wholeheartedly believe that we all must be encouraged to celebrate our uniqueness. How can we possibly be one hundred percent productive and happy at work otherwise? I believe that people should be nurtured with a raft of psychological support. Only then will true kindness flourish.

For me, it's all about the core values of honesty, authenticity and truth. So now, I have decided to wipe the whispered slate clean and come out all over again. I want people to learn from my story. I believe with every essence of my soul that kind, compassionate, wholeness is as fundamental as breathing. One cannot exist without the other. But without truth, these values are as disposable as a used tissue. Without honesty, these words are as forgettable as the well-meaning inclusion policies that fade into the background of political indifference. Without authenticity, my story is merely just that, a well-intended story. I am pig sick of watching some NHS leaders talk the talk by only paying lip service to inclusion without actually having the ability or even the commitment to walk the walk. So, it is now time to put my money where my mouth is by sharing my own lived experiences. Does my story come from a place of trauma? The answer is most definitely an unashamedly and unapologetically *yes*.

I stupidly thought that the Infirmary was my everything. I never imagined that she could slice me into pieces with the skill and precision of a heart surgeon. Personifying a hospital building was one of my gravest mistakes. It took me a couple of years of counselling to put this trauma to bed. Through my therapeutic journey, I have learnt that the Infirmary is no lady or all-encompassing protector. The hospital is just a collection of soulless Victorian buildings. I am now at peace with this discovery. Albeit, it has taken me thirty years to write this story. So when did my life start to unravel? I remember the events so clearly.

I was living my best version of life. Daniel made me blissfully happy, even if he did hate deep cleaning. Well, you can't be good at everything. Working as a qualified male midwife was enough for anyone.

"Now don't get too full of yourself, Daniel. Just remember that I am a hard act to follow. Did you not know that I was born on the maternity block where you have landed your first job?"

"I wondered why there is still a broken delivery couch and a pair of bent stirrups in the basement. How many midwives did it take to pull you out? I bet it was more like a game of tug of war. Your poor mother. You must have been such a bonny baby?"

The cheek of him. His conker eyes twinkled at me. But all of a sudden, things changed, and he abandoned me in an icy glaze. Wow, what a surprise to see him waiting for me after work. He was standing by the ward doors as I finished the late shift. In line with the natural order of being a student nurse, I was being predictively tormented by the one and only Sister Body. And what a body she had. Being only four feet tall and four feet wide, she wielded her compassion and force around the oncology ward with the sophistication and delicacy of Yoda in some Jedi training ritual. My survival plan was based on being acutely aware of where she was at any given time. As she stomped in one direction, I steered my course in the opposite. But these games were all wearing a little thin. This stupid carry-on belonged in comedy films and not in a modern-day hospital ward. Such archaic silliness was distracting me from learning. After all, I was there to train as a nurse.

Sister Body was a law unto herself. She was well known for making her cocktails of bowel opening and pain relief concoctions. I am sure she thought she was in a swanky Las Vegas lounge. She mixed and rattled her potions from her drugs trolley with the same flair as any bartender. Whilst not giving the patient the exact thrill of a Pina Colada or Exotic Daiquiri, her mixtures delivered the same medicinal effect. But when palliation was the only option, she served her finest cocktails. There is nothing sweeter tasting than a sip of kindness, a measure of love and a shot of tenderness as she soothed dying patients.

Many years later, fate intervened, and our paths collided again. This time, I didn't try to avoid her. When working as a community nurse, I found myself caring for the infirmaries' famous mixologist. Her immaculately kept bungalow was very much a reflection of her. There was order and cleanliness, attention to detail, and an unhurried sense of comfort. We chatted for many hours about the good old days of nursing over my visits. She chuckled with a glint of schoolgirl naughtiness as I told her that she terrorised me. The likes of Sister Jones, Sister Dickson and herself, had been cut from the same starched navy blue cloth. Smiling wryly, she explained that they were strict because that is how they were taught to behave. They simply knew nothing else.

Jane Body knew that she was dying. If anyone could recognise the signs after spending all of her career in oncology, then it was her. Her lung cancer was going to get her one way or another. Over her craft mat, oxygen and card-making antics, we sat one afternoon and developed her bespoke end-of-life care plan. Having such a distraction gave her the space to say exactly what she wanted. She even taught me how to layer decoupage roses in between making her wishes. Well, there was a first for everything. Although pretty, I couldn't imagine the hospice at-home team being overly impressed with a prescription covered in glitter. I'm sure that the doses of any anticipatory medication needed to be legible.

Jayne wanted to be at home when her big day arrived with Marie at the very centre of the party. Raising her eyebrows, she wheezed that Marie was her close friend. Choosing her cyanosed words carefully, she explained that there was no Mr Body as she had been solely married to her work. The two had met in the nineteen sixties over a drunk and disorderly patient. Being only a mere slip of a girl back then, Staff Nurse Jane took an instant like to PC Marie's command. They had been quietly intertwined ever since. Marie was a straight-talking, wiry-haired, slender creature. Armed in a cream pullover and sensible black slacks, there was no mistaking her presence as she walked into the room. She often finished Jane's sentences, as she struggled to talk through the hiss of the oxygen. They had travelled the world together.

"It's hard to believe it now, looking at her hiding behind that oxygen mask, throwing us daggers, but our infamous Sister Body here had no sense of danger in her younger days. You would have never thought that we rode camels in the Sahara, took a helicopter ride to the bottom of the Grand Canyon or went diving with sharks in the Great Barrier Reef. We have certainly lived. I suppose that is what happens when you work within oncology, doesn't it? Max, take some advice from that old battle-axe over there and drain every last drop out of life".

HOW CAN WE BE WRONG?

Marie squeezed Jane's hand. Through the corner of my eye, I caught a glimpse of Jane's ward sister glare. She knew exactly where this scowl had landed. Jane could still put shivers up my spine, even after all of this time. Breaking her stony silence, she then descended into a fit of giggles before coughing and reaching for the nebuliser machine. It was an absolute privilege to be part of the multidisciplinary team that made her last wishes come true. We all pulled together to make sure that Sister Body got anything that she wanted. This time, we weren't sending her on an exotic holiday. But for me, it was more rewarding to see her in comfort, relaxed and pain-free. With her beloved Marie holding her hand, I sadly served Jane a taste of her final cocktail. As she peacefully left this world for ventures new, I just simply sat and soothed her forehead with a damp flannel. She had done this so many times herself. As she took her final breath, I whispered a quiet 'thank you' in her ear. These two simple words said it all.

No broken leg was going to stop her. Even if it was pinned and wired like Darth Vader's latest weapon of destruction. At least this pigging metal contraption reminded her that she was still alive. That would teach her to go line dancing with Mavis. Next time, before jumping up so quickly maybe one less sherbet might be in order. Ouch, it hurt. The things she did for a bit of Achy Breaky Heart on a Saturday evening. The Jester cabaret club was her spiritual home, after all. Sadie was chief cook and bottle washer to the stars there for more years than she wanted to admit. Whatever they needed, she provided. It was the best job in the world. And the people she had met. It was an absolute honour to look after the likes of Roy Orbison, Tommy Cooper, Norman Wisdom, Cannon and Ball and Freddie Star, to name but a few. Not that she was one for name-dropping.

Cliff Richard was a perfect gentleman. They had broken the mould when they had made him. She gasped on entering the dressing room door with his favourite creamy tipple. It took her all of her strength not to wipe away a dribble of it above his top lip. Sadie was having a summer holiday all of her own as she watched him sup his cold milk, wearing only a pair of Union Jack boxer shorts. People would pay a fortune to be in her slingbacks. Not a single drop of alcohol ever touched those plump lips. He was as kind as he was handsome.

Sadie was torn. She couldn't decide if she liked Cliff or Cilla more. They were both beautiful in their own way. Cilla was the girl next door, Liverpudlian lass. She had no heirs and graces as she sat at the dressing table mirror. Bobby and Cilla chatted away with her like old friends every time they were in town. They never forgot to ask after her daughter Carla. Cilla laughed. She was so proud that Sadie was keeping it in the family. Well, the Liver Birds was written by Sadie's daughter's namesake. But Carla didn't want to be a writer. No, after watching a couple of episodes of Angels, she knew exactly what she wanted to do when she grew up.

Amethyst lampshades from the tables cast a glow of sophistication into the auditorium. You could hear a pin drop. The compare announced, 'We are pleased to welcome to the stage, the one and only Miss Cilla Black' and the audience went wild. A bottle of brown ale smashed to the floor in excitement. Sadie noticed this from her perch at the side of the stage. She summoned the bar staff, and it was gone before Cilla even had the chance to utter as much as a 'Hullo Chuck'. Cilla looked magnificent in white trousers, a silk black blouse and a silver waistcoat. She twinkled in the spotlight every time she moved. Sadie found it hard to believe that such a slender frame had the power to belt out her songs with such ease and grace. The very foundations of the club shook in admiration as she sang her hits and chatted to her audience as if she was swapping knitting patterns.

Sister Body caught the side of her consultant and sprang into action. She quickly pulled out the bone china tea service for Dr Taylor's ward round. Her finest royal Albert was reserved for him and him alone. His eyes twinkled when he saw his Jane sitting at her desk, attempting to write next month's work rota. She had tried every which way but loose, but still didn't have enough nurses to cover the shifts. George provided a welcome diversion to her predicament. They sat chit-chatting and sipped earl grey from the gilded rims, just like in the old days. From the privacy of her office, these friends were able to drop the formality that was expected by the junior staff. Taking a slurp, Jane piped up,

"How the devil are you George? I haven't seen you since my holiday. Is Maria Ok? I must give her a bell. There is many a time, I smile and think of your graduation. I vowed to myself that I would never wear a boned corset again for love nor money. It nearly bloody killed me. You would never guess what. I saw an article written by Dylan in a medical journal the other week. He is big in infectious diseases, somewhere in London. After all of these years, I thought he may have contacted one of us. Do you ever hear from him?"

"No Jane, I haven't heard from him. But anyway, how was your holiday? You don't do things by half, do you? All I want to do is to sit on a beach and read a book when Maria and I jet off. How was the Grand Canyon? I hoped that you stopped at Vegas for a flutter too?"

"The Canyon was amazing, thank you, George. I was nearly sick when the helicopter plunged to the base. Yes, we did do a stopover in sin city. It would be rude not to. Those fountains are amazing. I could have watched them all night long. Sadly, Marie had other ideas. It took me ages to prise her away from those slots. It was like she was possessed. But enough about me. How are those two strapping boys?"

"Christian is great, thanks. He is thinking of joining the family firm. We are looking at medical schools at the moment,"

"Well, he is a chip off the old block then, isn't he? How is Jack? I would love to see a photo of him in his RAF uniform. You must be so proud. Do you have one?"

And with that, Dr Taylor looked at his watch, took the last swig of his earl grey, threw on his white coat and asked Sister Body to join him for the ward round. It was time for work.

Sadie was going to get me hung. It was time for the dynamic duo to do their ward round. She patted the green counterpane and gestured me over to her bed. But Sadie wanted to talk rather than have her blood pressure taken. And who could blame her? Stuff it, let Sister Body do her worse. Before I knew it, Sadie had the whole bay of patients singing. *You're my world, you're my night and day. You're my world, you're every breath I take.* This was the medicine that she needed. *Other eyes see the stars up in the skies, but for me, they shine within your eyes.* And she did shine from beneath her shimmering silver nightgown and short auburn wig. With her arms stretched out in front of her she continued, *As the trees reach for the sun above, So my arms reach out to you with love.* She winked and allowed me to put the cuff on her arm. I had never taken someone's blood pressure before whilst they impersonated Cilla Black. I doubt it was very accurate either. But if it worked for Sadie, then it worked for me.

With all of the frivolity, I forgot to keep my eye out for the enemy. Sadie had only been transferred a few hours earlier, but she was already causing pandemonium. I had no idea that Sister Body and Dr Taylor were standing behind me at the notes trolley. Oh my god, I was in for it now. Before I had the chance to scurry away into the sluice, Sadie piped up,

"Now Sister, it's all my fault. You leave this poor student nurse alone. He was only doing what I asked him to."

I had no idea which way this was going to go. But hell froze over. Instead of a tongue-lashing, Sister Body smiled and said,

"Very well, Sadie, he has made an impression on you. Don't you worry, I have already had my supper."

Dr Taylor shuffled from foot to foot. He was desperate to finish his ward round before going home for the evening. This on-call business was for young men. I watched him run his hand through his receding blonde hairline. Our eyes met for longer than what was comfortable. In his prime, I bet that he had been quite a lady's man. Clearing his throat, he said,

"The orthopods have pinned this lady's leg up, but the bone cancer is not going anywhere soon. I'm just pleased that we have held her breast cancer at bay for all of these years. Sister, let's keep her comfortable now."

"Of course, Dr Taylor, you are the expert. Do you think we should increase her slow-release morphine dose? By the looks of her medication chart, she has had quite a few swigs of liquid stuff for breakthrough pain."

"Yes, Sister, once again you are right. Where would I be without you? Please pass me the medication chart and I will write it up myself before I go home. We can't have our own Cilla Black in pain, can we? Oh, and whilst I'm at it, I'll make sure that our star turn is written up for some laxatives too. This morphine business can play havoc with the old bowels."

And with this, the odd couple trundled past us and to the next patient. Sadie wanted to sit out in her bedside chair and wait for the night staff to arrive. She was not ready to be tucked up just yet.

Noticing the time, I gently placed my hand on her shoulder, smiled and said,

"Thank you for jumping in and saving me. Let's put it this way: I won't be needing any of your laxatives. Good night, Sadie, sweet dreams. We'll have to finish off the rest of the song in the morning. I can't wait."

It was such a surprise to see Daniel waiting for me at the ward doors. Even Sister Body smiled and said goodnight as we walked out into the autumn air. But something was wrong with him. There was no charm or kindness in his eyes. He hurried to his clapped-out old VW golf. I smelt fear. I waited for him to make eye contact with me, but he just stared blankly ahead. I could see his breath mist the windscreen, so he must have been alive. And then he spoke,

"Max, I don't know how to tell you this, so I'll just come out with it. I am HIV positive. The hospital has found out. Someone has told the media and we have to disappear for a while".

"What the fuck Daniel? You are joking, aren't you?"

But he wasn't. And just like that, everything changed. Hot vomit percolated in my throat. I couldn't hold it down. I watched in relief as the trail of sick merged and trickled into the dirty gutter water. Wiping the beads of cold sweat from the back of my neck, I coughed and attempted to compose myself.

We had just enough time to gather a few clothes before the media shitstorm began. The press circled like vultures ready to pick at our bones. In a trance, we drove away into the night. Daniel had gone from a male midwife to a demon in just one day. And now we were plummeting to hell together. None of this seemed real, but it was, and it was happening. We were living in the era of AIDS: Don't Die Of Ignorance fear-mongering HIV campaigns within Margaret Thatcher's Section 28 dogma. In the late eighties and early nineties, the LBGTQIA+ community were rightly demanding equality, much to the upset of so-called moral traditionalists. Section 28 was the Conservative government's response; Margaret Thatcher's answer to those who believed they have an inalienable right to be gay. This vaguely worded law prohibited local authorities and schools from promoting gay issues. It prevented councils from funding LBQTQIA+ initiatives. At a time when gay people were struggling to cope with the Aids epidemic, the conservatives attempted to suppress an already marginalised group. And now, here we were in the middle of it all.

Somehow, we had arrived at the Grand Elysian Hotel. This red-bricked Victorian pile was situated with stunning sea views over a rocky Cornish cliff face. The imposing building looked more like a lunatic asylum rather than a retreat. Maybe I would fit in well after all. But where were the strait jackets? I was convinced that we had been followed into the reception area. We picked a gay-owned hotel, thinking it would offer us purgatory. But this turned out to be a cruel mistake. Instead of feeling protected by our community, they banished us to our hotel room when the story broke in the national press. Even Blanche Dubois could rely on the kindness of strangers. To make matters worse, the hospital bosses told Daniel to sever contact with friends and family. God knows what was going through Danni's, Jack's, Kev's, and Aunt Bren's heads. We didn't know if and when we were ever going to return.

But luckily I wasn't alone after all. My golden friend was on hand to see me through. I didn't realise that he was waiting for me. He was the perfect partner to sit on the Laura Ashley bedspread together and sink deeper into nylon oblivion. What was that fucking noise? Had people been following us? Was that the click of a camera? Quick, shut the curtains so they can't see us. Good idea. Yes, it *was* Anna Ford talking about us. That wasn't in my head. Flickering images of us were being projected into our bedroom. Daniel was vilified but just sat quietly, watching it all unfold.

According to Anna, I was his willing moll. Distraught families were playing out their anger. Women gave first-hand accounts of their birth experience at the hands of this degenerate. HIV was a highly infectious illness with no cure and treatment in its infancy. With a careless needle stick injury or a slip of his episiotomy blade, Daniel could have delivered death into the world instead of life. Frankenstein's monster had to be found. The publicity pictures of Daniel were now being used to hang him. Good, kind people were whipped into a mass of hysteria and now demanded his soiled blood. I was as innocent as the mothers whom he had delivered. But the truth just didn't matter.

That's it, the voices were right. The gentle lapping of waves willed me on as I staggered down the wet slate. For a second, I stopped and wavered as the salt hit my face. But Danni, Jack and Aunt Bren were better off without me, anyway. If anything, I was doing everyone a favour. Music was playing loudly in my head. *Say it's only a paper moon sailing over a cardboard sea.* Being a fucking shirt lifter was a death sentence. *Yes, it's only a canvas sky hanging over a muslin tree.* Mrs Thatcher was right. *Without your love, it's a honkey tonk parade.* Let's laugh at the queer, that's all they are good for. Drizzle bit my cheeks. I was weightless; it was over. *Without your love, it's a melody played in a summer arcade.* No guiding light welcomed me to the other side. There was just darkness.

I woke up, face down at the side of the cliff, tasting sods of grass and vomit. I lay alone, cold, in more pain than I had ever experienced in all of my life, but for some reason, still alive. *It's a Barnum and Bailey world just as phoney as it can be.* Light pierced my eyes like needles. Daniel was awake and was waiting for me when I got back. He didn't ask where I had been. The dried vomit and soil spoke for themselves.

I couldn't stop shaking as I landed on the floor. Sobs of despair rang in the new day.

Once rested, cleaned and a little sober, Daniel and I spoke properly for the first time in three days. He said that he was in denial of his HIV status because it was a death sentence. In some parallel universe, he just wanted to make a difference in his life before it was over. He had put himself and everyone around him at risk. *It's phoney, it's plain to see how happy I would be if you believed in me.* I just couldn't get over that as much as I tried. A few days later we received contact from Dr Dent, the lead occupational health consultant at the City Infirmary. Now that things had blown over a little, we could return home. Our first port of call in the storm was the occupational health department. This was located on the third floor of the nurse's home. We walked along death row in silence on the way to our execution. If only I could turn back time. I would do anything to be cleaning the wooden panels instead of being shot up against them. Life was much simpler back then. I could smell the hospec hanging in the air. But this time, it offered only the scent of regret.

We shuffled into Dr Dent's office and sat down on two hard metal chairs. I then waited to be strapped in before the switch was flicked. I wasn't even asked if I had any last requests. Even the most heinous of murderers are offered this luxury before they are put out of their misery. There was an eerie quietness in the room. In these final moments, my eyes darted, trying to find something to fix my fear upon. I noticed a mahogany framed picture of Dr Dent with his wife and two grown-up children lovingly placed on his desk. Ironically, I recognised his son. He had been one of the many conquests that I had picked up from the gay scene. But that was in a previous life. I had smuggled him into my old room at the nurse's home only a few floors above. It was now his father's turn to fuck me over this time, good and proper.

Dr Dent, the director of nursing, the lead occupational health nurse, and the human resource manager sat at the other side of the table. Dr Dent cleared his throat and then broke the silence. He was a slender man in his early fifties. Dressed from head to foot in moth-balled tweed, he wielded his perfectly precise plum accent with equal measures of stifled disdain and disgust. His right eye twitched involuntarily as he spoke. Daniel was dismissed with immediate effect. He had brought the greatest shame in history upon the reputation of the hospital.

I watched Daniel from the corner of my eye. He didn't flinch. He was staring aimlessly through the window at the medical block. He seemed far more interested in a gaggle of excited student nurses who were on their way to work. I heard Tracey chatting with a porter and wished that I was outside with her. If only she knew what was going on within spitting distance. I doubt that she would have been laughing then. Although the infirmary had severed all connections with Daniel, hospital life carried on. He didn't utter a single word until he was asked directly if he understood what was happening to him. He replied with a monotone 'Yes'. But there is power in silence. He already knew his fate before taking us both into hiding, but just hadn't bothered to tell me. It turned out that I was just an annoying fly that had inadvertently landed in his ointment. And now I needed swatting.

My verdict was delivered by the director of nursing himself. He sighed and adjusted his black cap before speaking from beneath his moustache. I wondered if he recognised me. After all, it was only a few years ago since he had admired my ability to French polish. Today, I was forced into submission again. He had a terrible reputation and was well-known for doing anything to get what he wanted. But he hadn't had me. His kind of power was just a turn-off. The panel were so proud of themselves. They nodded, almost patting each other on the back when they unhatched my fate.

As casually as lighting a cigarette, Dr Dent produced a needle and syringe from his desk drawer. He began to label up the bottles in readiness to take my blood. Hang on a minute. What would happen if the results were positive? Would they let me back? Those questions were not up for discussion. By now, Doctor Dent had attached a needle to a syringe and was waiting for me to extend my arm. But I wouldn't let him near me. I staggered out of the death chamber and onto the hospital car park but for once I was not drunk. I had had HIV tests in the past and I knew that they were negative. But my word was not good enough. Only hard evidence would do. Daniel followed me and we left in silence.

Was anyone watching? Was that a click of a camera shutter or a postman pushing parcels through a letter box? I was frozen to the spot. Please, God, spare me a media blood bath. My prayers were answered there and then. The vultures had gone. Instead, we bumped into Larry, who lived in the flat above us. Although small in stature, he was wise in age. From beneath his grey dreadlocks and dilated pupils, he managed to slowly tell us that,

"There were people hangin' round the place for a few days asking all sorts of questions about you, man. I told them to go away and there was nothing to see. You two look fucked. Do you want a spliff? It's on the house."

I declined his offer and thanked him for his kindness all the same. I never imagined that our former den of seduction would provide the sanctuary that society could not offer. All I wanted to do was to retreat and find out who I was. Several messages were flashing on the answering machine, demanding our attention. But for now, I needed a hot soak with my bathroom ghost. He could watch if he wanted to. I was past caring. Sleep didn't come easily. It took a few slurps of lubrication to succumb to unconsciousness.

My head was cracking. Just how much whiskey had I guzzled the day before? I was still lying in the same sweaty position on the bed. Jesus, I stunk. I heard Daniel banging around in the kitchen. As I came too, the revolting stench of fresh coffee beans percolated around the flat. He knew I hated the smell of coffee, as it reminded me of my mother's stale breath. I just about made it to the toilet before wrenching my guts up. Right, next on the agenda was a cup of tea with just a drop of something in it to take the edge off my hangover. It must be five o'clock somewhere in the world.

As I sat sipping and stinking in my dressing gown, we talked. My breath stunk of vomit again, but I didn't care. If Daniel was happy to brew coffee, then I was happy to slur through sick-flavoured honesty. Everything about him looked the same, but I didn't recognise this man anymore. I didn't ask him if he loved me. That wasn't up for discussion today. I mustered empathy and care, but that is as far as it went. I was duty-bound to make this work as he had lost everything. I certainly didn't want his blood on my hands.

June, Daniel's mother, provided the litmus test for the wider reaction that I feared. Usually, she talked at one hundred miles an hour without taking a breath. But now she was screaming at him,

"You, you, and what have you done? Daniel, what have you done? Daniel, what have you done?! I'm your mother. I am the woman who brought you into this world. Why didn't you tell me? I had to find out from strangers knocking on my door in the middle of the night. Your father told them to bugger off. We have been hounded by reporters; I haven't been out of the house. I am so scared. I had no idea where you were and who you are. Why have you hidden this from me?"

And then she turned her attention to me.

"I have never liked you from the moment I met you. What have you done to my boy? You have infected him with this gay disease. You should have been boiled at birth. If only your mother had miscarried. You have given my son a death sentence. He was a good boy before he met you. I hope that you burn in hell, I hate you."

June was just hurt and confused. I thought that she was going to have a stroke as she shook in anger, clenching her fists and hyperventilating before collapsing into a chair behind her. She vented at me and I stood there and let her. When Daniel put her right, she crouched into the chair and sobbed. She looked up at me and said,

"I'm so, so sorry. I didn't realise that you didn't know either. I'm such a wicked woman. Can you ever forgive me?"

Before giving me the chance to reply she looked directly at Daniel and asked the question that had been on my lips for a few days.

"How long have you known Daniel?"

Daniel explained that he had been HIV-positive for just over a year. It would have been completely hypocritical to question his past. We were both major players on the gay scene in every which way that was humanly possible. It was just what many young, horny, gay men did. I had ridden the abundance of willing muscle Marys like a champion jockey. I had freed many a leather queen from their harness in my time, too. If it wasn't for Claire Raynor, then I could have easily been in the same boat as Daniel. Her dulcet tones of explaining how to don a condom on an erect penis had penetrated my sexual practice since entering the gay scene. Daniel told us that he had bare-backed a few times. Telling his mother this deserved a medal in itself. He certainly did not deserve condemnation. Many people had unprotected sex. The professional decisions that he subsequently made were a whole different kettle of fish, though.

My mind wandered again. I wanted to see Jack and Danni more than anyone else in the entire world. I believed in them, I trusted them, and I loved them. I didn't have to be Inspector Clouseau to work out that they would be angry with me. I had danced off into the moonlight without so much as an explanation or goodbye. June apologised over and over again as she drove me over to Jack and Paul's pad. I tried in vain to console her, but words were meaningless. It was good for Daniel to spend some time with his mother alone. Equally, I desperately wanted to be away from his grip for a while.

"Bloody hell fire. What on earth has happened to you, Max? We have all been out of our minds with worry. Where have you been? Why didn't you contact us? We phoned you over and over again, hoping desperately to hear your voice. We even went up to your flat, but were forced to make a sharp exit. News reporters were buzzing like flies around shit. Come on in, I'm so sorry, I'm just so relieved to see that you are still in one piece," Jack said whilst pulling me over the doorstep.

I was finally safe, resting my head next to his. Danni appeared from the kitchen and threw her arms around the scrummage. The tighter they gripped me, the more I cried. For now, that was all I needed. The crackle of the coal fire calmed my nerves until I was ready to speak. Regurgitating the events was as painful as it was surreal. It was as if I had been in my own melodrama. A while back, I watched the beautiful and haunting *An Early Frost*. This film tackled the subject of HIV and Aids. This poignant and powerful masterpiece is about a son who has to tell his parents that he is gay and has an Aids-related disease. I just never imagined that I would be living my version. Sometimes the facts are stranger than fiction. A mixture of Dolly Parton and booze lubricated the mood. Deep down, I knew that I needed to get another HIV test. It was the right thing to do. No one was going to be put at risk on my watch. But I wanted to do it under my own steam. In a world where so much had been out of my control, this was one thing that I could at least make a decision on. Whilst humming along to Dolly's *I Will Always Love You*, Jack volunteered to take me to the clinic the very next day.

The clinic was tucked away at the back of the outpatient department. It had its very own discreet entrance to hide its visitors from the general public's unwelcome glares. Clutching onto his hand for grim life, we stumbled up a few steps and carefully opened the grey door that led us into the waiting area. I had flashbacks of cleaning the clinic. But that was in a previous life. Although short in years, everything had changed now. The staff were warm, accepting and professional. They did not make me feel dirty or ashamed for being human. I could do that all by myself without any help. Mrs Thatcher and her cronies had already seen to that. Once examined, prodded and poked in all of the most delicate of places, it was time for my blood work to be completed. It was no less invasive than being exposed in the national press. If anything, it was easier. Following my consultation, I found Jack in the waiting room. He was engrossed in a copy of the Woman's Weekly whilst simultaneously shredding a plastic cup to pieces. I never realised that an article on the pros and cons of pressure cooking could provoke such a reaction. He was fighting with something in his head as we left the clinic. I knew that he was still annoyed with me for disappearing into thin air, but this was more. And then he said,

"Max, there is no right time for this conversation, but I need to tell you what is on my mind. Trust me, I get it. You didn't know about Daniel. You are a victim. But you don't have to be a martyr, too. You can choose. No one is making you stay with him. There, I have said it. I know it is not what you want to hear, and I'm sorry if I have upset you."

"I know that you are looking after me, Jack. To be honest, I have no idea how I feel about him. I just want to scream. For now, all I can do is take one day at a time and see what happens. I also feel guilty too. What happens if I leave him and he dies alone in some horrible hospital bed? I just can't get my head around it all."

"Well, whatever you decide, you know that I will be here for you. Just do me a massive favour, though. Before deciding to do a Houdini again, please tell me. My nerves just won't cope."

Jack put his arm around my shoulders as we walked toward his house. With Danni's advice still ringing in my head, I decided to make peace with Dr Dent. All I needed was a little time. My jigsaw pieces had fallen on the floor and I didn't know which one to pick up first. I could hear relief and a hint of regret in his voice. He told me that he was pleased to hear from me. He said that he was sorry for putting me on the spot. He too had got swept up in the hysteria. Sometimes people get things so wrong by just not thinking things through properly. I thanked him for his patience and kindness. A thousand thoughts went through my head when I put the receiver down. What would happen if I was HIV positive? Would I be allowed to finish off my nurse training? What would happen next? Was I going to live? Was I going to die?

Chapter Six

It was easier to exist in paralysis rather than to admit that love had left the building. Daniel stopped washing, changing his clothes, or even cleaning his teeth. Crusts of spit hung around his beard, but he didn't care. And neither did I. It was easier to sleep on the couch than be near him. He stunk anyway. Would he just stop playing that bloody song over and over again? Any of us could wallow in Annie Lennox's *Why* if we wanted to. He lay on the floor, staring at the ceiling, mouthing the words over and over again. I was in no mood for a pity party. Was he *viciously unkind*? It wasn't a question that I was willing to think about. But it was obvious that *this boat was sinking*. But I wasn't a monster, was I? He wouldn't die alone. I had seen too many of those Don't Die of Ignorance TV campaigns to be that callous. No tombstone with his name on it would be popping up in our front room if I had anything to do with it. But his life wasn't over. He couldn't be a midwife, but nothing was stopping him from licking his wounds and getting a job as a staff nurse somewhere out of the area. Dr Dent hadn't completely destroyed him. But no, this wasn't good enough for the gay glitterati that had fallen from grace. He never once considered that my fate was still hanging in the balance.

I heard the telephone receiver quickly clunk down. He realised that I had entered our flat.

"Who are you talking to Daniel? That receiver is hot under your face. You must have been on for ages. Are you keeping BT in business?"

"No one important, Max. Just someone I know, that's all."

"Well, for someone who isn't important, you have certainly been on the blower for a long time."

He looked sheepish. What was he up to now? He had always had his own circle of friends. Up until this point, none of that bothered me. I wasn't his keeper, after all. It took me all of my strength to remain calm. Why did he end the call so abruptly? As soon as he left the room to make a coffee, I called 1471 to get his last dialled number. A man's voice with a thick Scottish accent answered, laughed and said,

"Hi Daniel, haven't you had enough of me already for one day? You will get caught if you carry on."

Slamming down the receiver in anger, I dug out the last phone bill statement and saw that he had been chatting to this man for hours on end. I was shaking, but there was no way that I was going to show this bastard that I was bothered. Well, if it was sauce for the goose, then it was sauce for the gander. I couldn't look at him for fear of giving the game away. Instead, I took half a bottle of my friend into the bathroom, locked the door and ran a hot steaming bath. I could always rely on his golden advice to see me through. Both the bathroom ghost and my liquid lover chatted as I soaked.

"Just do what you do best, Max. Slap your war paint on and prize yourself into those white ripped shorts. They are still hidden in the back of the closet. You know that they show off your bubble butt so well. No man can resist you in them. Put on that lumberjack shirt and strut out of this fucking flat with your head held high."

And that is exactly what I did. Before slamming the door behind me, I turned, cocked my head, and quickly ran a finger down my torso.

Daniel didn't say a single word when he saw me dressed and ready for battle. He would have plenty of time to phone his jock now. Before I knew it, I found myself cruising in Queen's Park. It wasn't long before I was face down, smelling of grass and semen whilst Queen Victoria looked on. Old habits die hard.

"Max, Max, Max, Max, it's your turn. You are miles away. What's going through that head of yours?"

"You don't want to know, Jack."

He frowned at me. Luckily the consulting door swung open before Jack had the chance to take the conversation any further. Everything rested upon the decision waiting behind door number three. But this wasn't a game show. I was ushered into the cubicle and almost collapsed in anticipation of the results. Nurse Sally tried desperately to give me a speech about safe sex. It was probably a good job that she didn't know where I had been the night before. When I looked down, I still had scratch marks on my arms from climbing out of the bushes. What the fuck had I done? I nodded in all the right places, like one of those obedient dogs that you find in a car's rear window. I wasn't listening to her well-meaning pre-amble. In my head, I was screaming, 'Just get on with it and tell me one way or another. It's all right for you, sitting there in that lovely staff nurse uniform. At least you have had the chance to wear one. You know nothing about me or what I am capable of.' And then she stopped banging her gums. Please, for God's sake, get to the point. Well, that was a bolt from the blue; the HIV test was negative.

I was stunned. Instead of feeling relief, I was overwhelmed. Instead of feeling happiness, I wept. My HIV status wasn't the problem. I had already contracted a terrible disease, anyway. There was just no cure for stigma and bigotry. And why the hell had I listened to those bathroom friends of mine? I was lower than a snake's belly.

Jack was waiting in the reception room, slowly crushing the life out of a plastic water cup again. That was marginally better than indulging in a Woman's Weekly. He did what he always did and scooped me up in his arms. But this was no romantic blockbuster where the boy always gets the girl at the end of the movie. On leaving the clinic, we walked to the outskirts of the hospital and collapsed upon a flaky green bench under an old oak tree, sitting hand in hand for a while and admiring the view of the nurses' home and car park. I told him that my test was negative and caught a tear with my finger that was rolling down his cheek. For once, he was silent.

With the bit firmly clasped in between my teeth, I went back to nurse training. I was going to rise, even if it hurt like hell. This was a real baptism of fire. Adrenaline coursed through my veins as I made my way towards the classroom. Maybe just a swig of something to take the edge off would help. Damn it, I had left my friend at home. I stumbled into an 'ethics of nursing' session. Sam flicked the switch to his overhead projector and slapped a poorly written laminate down.

When Joan Jangles....

...nothing happens. When Joan jangles what is she trying to say? When she rasps toward staff in sodden sallowness what does she need? No, what does she need beyond the functionality of her pad change and some well-meaning patronisation, but it is patronisation all the same. She is not a child after all. Telling her to sit down just makes her worse. Lost in her loneliness, all she can do is jangle.

A bouffant of bedraggled backcombed hair is just hot in her neck. Gone is her hedgehog cut and in are these foreign curls. She had spent a lifetime in joggers and T-shirts, so why wouldn't she remove the straight jacket that she has now been dressed in? They can't belong to her, can they? The sensibly pleated black nylon skirt and floral blouse are as alien to her as that damn music that is relentlessly repeated from the dayroom speaker. There is just no escape from this loop of disjointed disconnection. At times, she succumbs and sits sobbing and slobbering in this circle of diabolical despair. But the music still plays on. And then she doesn't jangle. No, then she is quiet.

But why does Joan Jangle? If only Bella hadn't gone. She searched and searched but still couldn't find her. Bella was her love, her life, her everything. A montage of memories was thrown out as easily as lowering Bella's coffin into the unwelcoming ground. Nothing was saved for comfort or care. Gone was the record of a life spent together. Pictures of their Vegas wedding where Elvis had driven them in his pink Cadillac through the strip were destroyed in a blink of an eye. Cracked vinyl of their favourite bands was thrown out as easily as yesterday's newspapers. Thirty-five years of love letters were dispensed with no thought. Nigel had fed their love into the welcoming skip and watched as the metal jaws chomped it away. He was ashamed that his cousin had been living that way. But that didn't stop Joan from jangling.

Through his round glasses, short-cropped hair and scissored hand gestures, Sam asked his young student nurses a few leading questions.

"Now class, why do you think that Joan jangles? Is it her dementia or something else? Were the nurses right to let this happen? What would have you done if you were the nurse on duty? Is there anything that we can do differently? What do you think of Nigel? Now get yourselves into groups of three or four. I'll give you thirty minutes for you to plan your collective responses and feedback to the larger group..."

And then I interrupted him in mid-flow. Every eye in the room pierced into me. But there was no going back. A student nurse whispered,

"What is that Aids fucker doing here...he needs to fuck off and die."

She was only saying what everyone else was thinking. And then, instead of hate, I was met with ginger ringlets of kindness. Tracey leapt to her feet.

"Will you shut up or get out? You are the problem here, not Max. Have you not been listening to the last thirty minutes of our class? What part of the providing non-judgemental care bit can you not get into that ugly fat head of yours?"

The room was filled with a quiet ripple of cheer. Tracey sat down and eyeballed my abuser until she retreated under her stone. I didn't know that Tracey had it in her. Kev pulled up a chair next to him and beckoned me over. This was just the start of the abuse that would follow me onto the wards.

I braced myself for the worse and the hospital certainly didn't disappoint. Where there should have been compassion, there was hate. Where there should have been understanding, there was disgust. Unless it was work-related, no one wanted to speak to me. I got all of the rubbish shifts. I tried desperately not to ring my leper bell too loudly. All of a sudden staff had their own cup with their name on it. They didn't even let me use the same toilet. I could hear people talking about me while I tried to work,

"Yes, that's him. He's the one with Aids. Who let him back here? He doesn't belong with us."

God knows how I was going to get through alive and in one piece. It was like standing at that cliff edge all over again. And then things just got worse. The ward staff would not allow me to take breaks with them. The staff canteen was my only alternative other than standing out, exposed to the elements. And my body just couldn't cope with double pneumonia. This coldly calculated act meant I was further exposed to the wider hospital community. The room went quiet when I tried to slip in undetected. Everyone stared at me in horror.

I swallowed hard. It was a struggle to hold down anxiety and vomit simultaneously. Droplets of beaded sweat on my forehead warned me that I was about to keel over any second. No one would serve me. Well, I suppose that I should be thankful for small mercies; I wasn't hungry, anyway. They didn't want me to contaminate the food or utensils. The clatter of plates and frivolity of chatter ended abruptly when I tried to sit down with Carla and Vivien. They looked through me as if I didn't exist. Just as I was being cold-shouldered a voice bellowed above the commotion. A bolt of blonde, curly lightning came to my rescue.

"That is my nephew you are all bloody talking about! Just what do you think you are doing? He has done nothing wrong! It's not his fault, you horrible bunch of evil bitches. You callous cows! He isn't contagious, not that you lot care, anyway. And you call yourself nurses. You are a disgrace to what it stands for."

And with that, she grabbed hold of my arm and led me out. Aunt Bren was hyperventilating. I had not seen her this angry since her fight with Rita. Once in control of her breath again, she hatched a survival plan. She turned up on the wards and threw daggers if anyone dared to put one foot out of line. And it worked like a dream. I was completely in awe of the measures that she went to protect me. With folded arms and a tapping foot, she made her presence known. If only I could borrow her armour to carry me through the last few months of nurse training. And then I realised that I needed to mould my own if I was to survive.

Chapter Seven

The shimmer of the lava lamp cast an aura of enchantment within her boudoir. She slumped her derriere upon the padded velvet chair next to her altar and prayed to the god of mascara for a miracle to happen. Through a plume of cigarette smoke, Bren shook her head at the sight of her invading roots. She pulled back her split ends and secured them in place with an Alice band. And then she went into battle once again. She wanted to look her best when her nephew visited later. This was a big day for Max. It wasn't every day that you found out if your nephew had qualified as a nurse. But this task was becoming more of an uphill struggle. Pilfering through her pots of potions, powders and paints suddenly reminded her that she must pay her ding dong lady. After all, Avon had been her lifeline over the years. If only she had kept those empty perfume bottles from the nineteen seventies; she would have been dripping in real gold by now. It would have paid for at least a facelift. Oh well, some things are just not meant to be.

She flicked the switch and turned on the white bulbs that glowed around her mirror. It was showtime. Much to her disgust, she now saw her forty-odd years of life reflected back to her. But her wrinkles weren't laughter lines. Every single one of them told a story of their own. And where had these bloody crow's feet come from? She caught a glimpse of the room behind her as she powdered, puffed and puckered herself into her version of perfection. *And once again, it was time to be someone else who was anyone but her.* The colour purple was her absolute favourite thing. It represented anything to anyone. Some people associated the colour with stately royal robes, others with death and some even with spiritual awakening. And Bren knew that she was all of them mixed up in her beautiful quandary. Sumptuous lilac dripped from the walls onto the tufted amethyst shag. The tones of velvet-padded plum had welcomed many a gentleman caller into the delights of her wrought iron four poster. Both Bren and the bed frame shared the same metal fatigue. She had spent many of an hour counting the shimmering stars above her head. They were embossed into the canopy of violet voile that hung above her lair. She even remembered to whimper and pant in all of the right places as the faceless men wriggled and writhed on top of her. But none of this transitory relief came close to filling the deep hole that bore inside her. Within the secret reaches of her yearning, all that Bren wanted was peace.

Try as she might, she could not find Mr Right. The problem was that no one could hold a candle to her Tony. That day still haunted her. Every time she closed her eyes, she could see him lying in his coffin before he was burnt. It was barbaric to identify his body before he was pushed into the crematoria. She could still feel the heat on her face and the crackle of the welcoming furnace as it lunged into life. As much as she tried to understand, Spanish cremation rituals were not for her. Footloose and fancy-free, they had left the UK on a whim to run a small caravan park within the hills of Malaga only three years previously. Navigating the rudiments of the Spanish health service was never part of the deal. They discovered that the universal language of lung cancer has no translation barriers. This disease just devoured everything within its rasping path. Tony was too frail to move in the end; the flight back home would have killed him. Alone in that hot tin box, with little support, Bren did her best to nurse her husband. In her mind's eye, she could still smell the meaty stench of cancer on her Tony's breath. No amount of perfume could camouflage the unmistakable smell of death. It was almost a relief when Tony finally took his last wet breath in the stillness of that hot caravan. Rather than paradise, this move had turned into hell.

Damn it, where was that waterproof mascara brush? Her face was ruined again. She foraged for her best make-up to blend the tears away. But what could Bren do? As long as the world was still turning, there was no choice but to carry on. She had returned to the UK, clutching her suitcase in one hand and Tony in the other. She wasn't going to leave him in Spain, even if they did stop her at customs, as his metal urn had been picked up on the x-ray machine. Bren thought about where to scatter Tony and then needed to apply a little more mascara. Maybe she would take him to the grounds of his hallowed football stadium for one last time or to the same churchyard where they had married. But for now, he was placed beside her bed at the back of a rickety wardrobe. Her sister, Karen, had conveniently arranged her rental flat within staggering distance of the hospital. Karen had even sweet-talked her boss, Mrs M, the domestic supervisor, into giving Bren a job too. Bren and Karen would scrub and polish the hospital together.

Putting it bluntly, they were bound together by the commonality of childhood trauma. In her heyday, their mother Annie thought of herself as a bit of a catch. Bren had studied her worshipping the dressing table mirror on many an occasion. She watched this woman apply just a little too much rouge to pass for respectable, just a little too much mascara to pass for expensive and just a little too much cruelty to pass for actually giving a damn about her children. Both Sisters were no strangers to the reality of hard work. Annie had farmed them out to run errands and skivvy as soon as they could walk. The cost of their mother's beauty had to be paid for one way or the other. When not bleeding their fingers to the bone, the girls were left to care for their three younger brothers. Annie didn't care if any of her five children were hungry or not. She didn't care if they lay in soiled beds, crying themselves to sleep at night. Her main priority in life was to keep hold of her husband Sid before he disappeared with one of his numerous floosies. Sid wasn't fussy at all. Everyone knew that if it had a pulse, then he would try to shag it. And if it didn't have a pulse, then he would shag it anyway until it did. Annie always looked so glamorous with her lacquered crimson beehive, her painted cheekbones and matching lipstick. In reality, she was just plain old mutton dressed as lamb. In time-honoured tradition, the other women within the terraced row proudly washed the coal dust from their windows, whitened their net curtains and reddened their doorsteps. Standing with crossed arms, they muttered 'jezebel' under their breath as Annie tittered past in her fake fur coat. She had even perfected the art of tittering in four-inch stilettos across the cobblestones. But no amount of knockoff finery could hide the fact that she was just rotten. These house-coated women saw her for what she was; a sow's ear and never a silk purse.

Bren felt special for the first time in her life. Annie smiled as they sat together peering into the dressing table mirror. She was even allowed to caress her mother's most precious possessions. In awe, Bren ran her cold finger through the assortment of pencils, powders, and paints that lined the worn mahogany top. The horsehair makeup brush caressed her pubescent skin. She fell in love with the firm texture of the nylon mascara brush as it willed her long lashes into submission. And then she stared out from behind her smoky purple eyes in sheer amazement. Yes, Mother was right; crimson was the right shade of lipstick to complete her makeover. She coughed on the mist of hairspray that held her golden locks in place. Bren then slipped into one of her mother's cast-offs. The snugness of a tight black PVC pencil skirt felt at odds against her soft thighs. A low-cut purple blouse hung over her black satin bra. Bren was so lucky that she inherited her mother's hourglass figure. Like Dr Frankenstein, Annie held her daughter's jawline and briskly moved her head from side to side. She grinned and studied her creation in the mirror. To her relief, she had managed to do something with the wench after all. She would go down well by the time Annie had finished tarting her up.

Bren shook, but didn't dare to move. She was pinned to the red leather on the back seat of this white Ford Cortina. This brill creamed brute was hurting her but didn't seem to care. His industrial hands mauled her body in disregard. The weight of his sweaty body crucified her as she cried for it to be over. And then he grunted and panted on top of her in his beer-stained shirt and half-mast overall trousers. Bren did her best to imagine that she wasn't there, even if her pain was shaking her. Catching a glimpse of the upholstery over his shoulder, she counted the dots that were imprinted within the vinyl ceiling of the car. She smelled the stale beer on his breath as he pushed himself further into her before finally exploding and groaning.

This punter was going to get his money's worth and had even paid extra to break her in. Bren wept silently as she bled into a pair of second-hand black knickers. Now that this man had finally done with her, she slithered off his back seat. With blood trickling down her leg she staggered in the general direction of her mother. That would be the first and last time that Annie would show her the ropes. From now on, come rain or shine, Bren would work the canal alone. She learnt that she could make a packet every Friday at lunchtime. When men's balls were full as the notes that were stuffed in their greasy overall pockets, it was easy pickings as they fell out of the pub and into her.

As Bren sat, she turned up her trannie just a little bit more. She smiled as the tune of *Je Taime Moi Non-Plus* drifted over the airwaves and into her perfect purple palace. The song took her right back to sixty-nine; both her favourite year and number. If only she had a pound for every time she had played that scratched seven-inch. From working the canal for years, she knew what men really wanted. A year or two after leaving school, these skills were put to good use when she landed a job as a barmaid at the Potter's Arms.

Tony had compared her to a poor man's Barbara Streisand without the beak or voice. What a chat-up line. By trade, he was a porter at the City Infirmary. He often stumbled into the pub where Bren was working. His beerometer as he called it, improved with every pint he drank. After five pints he was any-ones and after six, he was even Bren's. The cheek of him. He had the knack of flattering her with hilarious but harmless backhand compliments. This larger-than-life lad didn't demand anything from her. He stood at around five and a half feet tall, in his faded denim jacket and bell-bottom jeans or six feet when wearing his platform boots. But it wasn't long before he wheedled a place right into her heart. He was required to tie up his hair for work, but when let loose, his auburn long locks danced a melody all of their own. As she got to know him, she learnt exactly when he was about to cast one of his wisecracks. He flicked his fringe to one side to show an unmistakable twinkle in his emerald eyes. Bren just felt comfortable in his freckled company. This was a breakthrough in itself, considering her less-than-perfect past. A year later they were married and living in the rented flat above the pub.

She was the Jane Birkin to his Serge Gainsbourg in every which way that was humanly possible. *Je t'aime, je t'aime, Oh oui, je t'amime.* It was such a shame to see it go to waste when so many other people could benefit from the heat that burned within their wet loins. *Moi non plus, Oh mom amour.* And this is how Bren and Tony entered the swinging scene without so much as a pampas grass on the verge outside the pub. *Comme la vague irresoule, Je vais, je vais et je vais.* They were doing no harm and, if anything, they provided a public service. With Tony holding his rod firmly in his hand, he cast his net far and wide within the pool of staff at the hospital. He was no stranger to inviting his familiars as he called them, back to the pub after work. After a few drinks to lubricate the mood, it was easy to retire to the delights of the upstairs flat. *Entre tes reins, Je vais et viens.* Sometimes his catch of the day was a fellow porter or domestic assistant. With more patience, Tony even managed to lure nurses and doctors into Bren's fish nets. It never failed to impress them with what went on underneath their respectable starched hats and stiff white coats. George, a blonde-haired doctor, was a repeat visitor. It was ironic that such a randy young man wanted to be an oncologist. For some reason, he favoured the delights of Tony more than Bren. And just as long as everyone was happy, anything went.

In the corner of her dressing table mirror, Bren spotted a few grainy photos of her family. Her eyes rested on a battered picture of Karen and her standing by the outside privy. In this backdrop of deprivation, endless plumes of smog billowed relentlessly from the melting pot of heavy industry. She still remembered their thankless task of hanging up the hearth rug on the clothesline and beating it to death. That soot just got everywhere. She remembered the scurry of mice that ran across the picture rails within the scullery. The more they tried to poison them, the more they just seemed to breed. As Bren studied the old photo, her eyes rested upon Karen. She found it so hard to understand her sister's behaviour lately. Max was just Max, her lovely young nephew. It didn't matter to her if he was gay, straight or anything else in-between. Her sister cared more about what the neighbours would say rather than the welfare of her son. You could take the bitch out of the slum, but you couldn't take the slum out of the bitch. Just because she had got her a job at the City Infirmary on her return from Spain, didn't make her a bloody saint. Wrong is wrong, no matter how you try to dress it up as something else.

Bren didn't understand the reality of her sister's life any more than she knew why she had kept hold of her Tony's ashes. As it turned out, Annie had been an expert at divide and conquer at all costs. She was more than happy to turn a blind eye to anything that she didn't want to see. Bren had no idea what her older sister had endured under that diabolical roof, too. Equally, Bren was too ashamed to tell her sister about working the canal. If only they had confided in each other instead of competing for attention, life could have been so different.

Karen didn't want to breathe in case she wet herself again. She never closed her eyes in case he was on top of her again when she awoke. She did her cat napping on the days when she went to school. She dreaded the sound of his familiar footsteps on the stairs and the creak of her bedroom door opening. His heavy hand muffled her whimpers as he did those things. It was even rougher when he was drunk. So she lay in silence, hoping he didn't hear her cry. It didn't stop until he shuddered and left her in slimy wetness. Karen had no idea what was going on at first. No, she was only twelve when it started. And when she did understand, it was too late, as no one would believe her by then.

The dirty bitch had been letting the boys at school poke her. Yet again, Annie was left to pick the pieces up. That slut of a daughter couldn't keep her knickers on. One way or another, she would pay for this. Karen lay on the kitchen table as dirty newspapers crinkled beneath her. There was still blood on it from this butcher's last victim.

She hadn't even qualified for a clean sheet, let alone an anaesthetic or hospital care. According to her mother, no one needed to know just what a horrible lying whore her daughter had turned into. Karen could smell the hate on her mother's breath as she spat,

"You had this coming. This is exactly what happens to filthy, lying sluts like you. How could you say these things about your father?"

Karen saw the dirty crochet needle looming towards her and then reluctantly lifted her legs. All she remembered before she passed out was searing agony as the hook ripped inside her. Somewhere between the living and dead, she limped back through the back alleys in a blood-soaked splat. An old rag had been shoved in between her legs to catch the livery clots as she tried to stagger home. Annie made it clear to her that she would not be allowed through the front door in that sorry state. As Karen finally found the peeling back gate, she didn't care if she lived or died. Nothing was worse than this. Annie ushered her into the outside privy before anyone saw her. Karen spent the night alone in the toilet, holding onto the rough walls as her only comfort. She was shivering and then burning, vomiting and then wrenching, haemorrhaging and then convulsing. She stayed there until all evidence of the baby had been flushed away. But there was a God; Father never touched her again.

Karen was on her way to work at the local clothing mill when she bumped into Alan. He couldn't miss her in her mother's cast-off green PVC raincoat. There was something special, innocent, and sweet about her. She was a bird of paradise that needed to be protected. Alan was her knight in shining winkle pickers and purple teddy boy suit. It didn't take long to whisk her away to a life of respectable catholic bliss. After the white wedding, the couple lived with Alan's mother, father and two sisters. It was a tight squeeze, rubbing along together in a three-bedroom council house. But they just got on with it. For the first time in her life, Karen was safe. Alan's father, Max, gently teased the newlyweds through his southern Irish lilt on every occasion possible. On one occasion, Max asked the newlyweds to put a pillow in between the headboard and the wall as no one else could sleep. But their attempts to conceive a child were fruitless. A gynaecologist was consulted. Following an examination, the couple were delivered some devastating news that no newlyweds or otherwise wanted to hear. The damage at the hands of the back street butcher had shredded any chances of a baby. But he was wrong as a couple of years later, little Max arrived. Karen stared at her baby's beautiful face through the clear plastic cot in the swanky new maternity ward and was sure of only one thing. She would give her son everything that she had never had growing up. Nothing or no one would come between them. She cried in amazement as he wrapped his tiny pink hand instinctively around her finger.

Ta-da, Bren was finally ready. The time had just run away with her again. A drag queen would take less time to get ready. She had been sitting at her dressing table for over an hour and had a numb bottom to prove it. A sly smile crept from the side of her crimson lips as she checked herself in her mirror. Somehow she had managed to do it again. She almost looked respectable, not completely, but almost. She just had time to clip the rhinestones in her ears and slap on her smile for all occasions. Max didn't need to see her panda eyes on graduation day after all. Bren just hoped that he had got some good news for a change.

Chapter Eight

It was finally graduation day. My future was sealed in a rather non-descript brown envelope at the reception desk at the Department of Nursing. Don't get me wrong, I wasn't exactly expecting a fanfare as I pushed the fingerprinted glass doors open for one last time. But this was just a soulless way of finding out my fate. Especially as the last three years of blood, sweat, and tears had nearly destroyed me in the process. A frenzy of excited relief echoed around the reception, as one by one my fellow students were handed letters. Tracey and Kev had both qualified. I was overjoyed for them. And then it was my turn. Breathing heavily, I opened the letter, almost not daring to look at the results. I read the print over and over again in disbelief. I had done it. Danni and Jack caught hold of me from each side before I landed on the corduroy tiles. Where would I be without them? A carpet burn wasn't the look that I was going for. For the first time in a few months, I was genuinely happy, but now also a little giddy. Still elated, I bounded into our flat like a naughty puppy, waving my letter at Daniel above my head like a pride flag. I expected something but received nothing. I might as well of told him that we had run out of milk. I had finally had enough of the bastard. And just like that, I told him to pack his bags, take Annie Lennox with him and go. It was over.

I could almost pass for normal. The coolness of the blue suit glided over my peaks and troughs. In contrast, a white shirt collar stood to attention, chaffing my neckline. A paisley tie slithered around my throat, almost choking me. Black patent leather shoes with a hint of a Cuban heel completed the look. Trying to suck in my beer pouch, I stood side-on in my bedroom mirror. Bloody hell, there were still a few remnants of my badly bleached quiff, but I had run out of time to do anything more now. A lumpy knock at the door interrupted my annoyance.

Jack pirouetted in mid-air whilst trying to take his trainers off. How had he survived RAF training? Judging by his lack of coordination, I couldn't see him with anything more menacing than a fish knife. He stared up and gasped,

Oh my god Max, doesn't she scrub up well? You big butch thing you, go, girl, go Florence. Now, don't be hiding behind that suit Max, you are as good as anyone else."

He was the king of pep talks. He had just compared me to her Royal Highness of the Lamp. The pressure was killing me. How could I live up to such praise, especially after everything that had happened? Danni had sold her soul to the devil and set up this staff nurse interview for me in the neuroscience unit, and I didn't want to let her down. But I was losing my bottle and no matter how much I tried to forget, I could still feel Stanley Kowalski's grip on me. Jack moved his head from side to side and sputtered,

"Well, let's have it sugar tits? Now listen to me and let's get one thing straight... well actually it will be the only thing that's straight in this room, won't it? You can do this, believe me. I am desperate to see you mince down that ward in a pair of blue epilates glistening from your shoulders, if it is the last thing that I do."

"Come here, Jack, and give me a hug, you big lump. What would I do without you? But don't crease me, whatever you do."

He was right. I had nothing left to lose. I put all of my money on red twenty and span the interview roulette wheel. Jack described this as my 'epiphany in Tiffany moment'. With a bit of Lady Luck, maybe I could hit the interview jackpot.

Senior Sister Sharron Varley and Junior Sister Jackie Hensley beamed in navy kindness as I sat down. My left leg seemed to have a mind of its own and refused to stop shaking. Sister Sharron sported a striking black glossy pageboy haircut and rich hazel eyes. I had done my homework, and Danni told me that she had risen to the position of ward sister in her thirties through hard work and dedication. It was a case of what you see is what you get with her. Her trusty sidekick, Junior Sister Jackie was a blonde bombshell. This pinup would have not looked out of place on the front cover of *Vogue*. Together, they formed a Cagney and Lacey double act.

"We are going to make this interview as painless as possible, Max. We want to bring out the best in you, so take a deep breath and relax. We won't eat you, I promise," Sister Sharron laughed before the formal questioning began.

If I am honest, the interview was a blur. I have no idea what they asked me. But Sister Sharron stunned me before I reached for the door and stumbled out. Slowly curling her top lip, her words slipped effortlessly through her crimson lipstick.

"Max, we take on any waifs or strays here, if we think they are any good, of course, we are not fussy."

I sat glued to the telephone and willed it to ring. One way or the other, I needed to be put out of my misery. My life flashed before me as the telephone finally rang.

"Hi, Max, it's Sharron Varley. I'm calling to discuss your interview today. I just wanted to say that we would love to have you on our team. We think that you are a diamond in the rough. We can smooth your edges and make you shine. We would formally like to offer you the job of Staff Nurse within our neuroscience ward, do you accept?"

I had done it. I told her that I desperately wanted the job. Sharron laughed and then welcomed me to her nursing family.

"For the sake of the Virgin Mary, Mother of Jesus, can you please put me out of my misery and tell me what she bloody said? Have you got the job? This is just too much for my fragile nerves to cope with."

I stumbled into Jack's outstretched arms. We were both shaking like leaves when I told him that it was a yes. And then he kissed me.

Chapter Nine

Like Cinderella just before midnight, I glided towards the sewing room. Through the dark corridors, I could hear the gentle serenade of the singer sewing machines getting louder and louder. I caught sight of my fairy godmother through the door. I could smell the yards of starched nylon as I crossed the threshold. I smiled sweetly and greeted her.

"I'm here again Maggie. I'm hoping that you can produce a miracle and make me look like a respectable staff nurse. For some strange reason, I have landed a job with Sister Varley and her team. Can you believe it? I'm still pinching myself. Can you get your wand out please and work your magic? I think I may need a bigger size than my student nurse tunic, sorry."

Maggie didn't smile. She appeared to be distracted, telling me that she didn't do 'bibbity, bobbity, boo' for anyone, with or without a wand. Once she had donned a pair of disposable gloves and an apron, she measured me up. Maybe it was a new hospital infection, prevention and control measure that had been introduced. It was just easier to say nothing. Once she had completed my silent fitting, she disappeared into her cage. She returned with five white crisp tunic tops and five pairs of navy creaseless trousers, in a size just a bit bigger than I had worn before. She then fumbled through her perfectly labelled wooden draws and produced her final offering. To her, it was just a pair of light blue staff nurse epilates, but to me it was everything.

Why were so many important decisions made over the din of the gay scene? I could hardly hear her words over the dulcet tones of Right Said Fred's *I'm too sexy* as Danni mouthed into my ear,

"So what is the plan of attack, Max? Getting those blue epilates is one thing, but living up to them is a whole new ball game."

Of course, she was right, she always was, even if it was difficult to make any sense of her. I had put all of my focus into surviving the last year of student nurse training through 'damage limitation'. It never occurred to me that I would get a job. Through cider-infused good intentions, she slurred,

"Don't worry, Max, it's just like learning to drive. You don't learn to do it properly until you have passed your test. I will help you. After all, I am teaching student nurses now, aren't I?"

Then she grabbed my hand and led me through the oblivion of dry ice and onto the dance floor. We landed in the nameless scrum of silhouettes that gyrated to Erasure's '*I Love to hate you*'. Through the giddy haze of Calvin Klein jock straps and the stench of hot bodies and poppers, I became distracted. Was that Jack and Paul arguing by the bar? Jack had not mentioned Paul lately. In fact, he rarely mentioned him at all.

Squeaking through the sweat, we sliced through the dance floor and found Jack sobbing into his beer. He crouched like a coiled spring, where one wrong move would see him explode. A strobe light hit his face to reveal the reality of abuse.

"Whatever has gone on, Jack? Who has done this to you? I will kill them," I screamed, before coming to my senses and soaking up his blood with my T-shirt. "We need to get you cleaned up properly before we do anything else, it looks like those cuts are deep, they have barely missed your eyes."

By now there was a crowd of onlookers gathering around the crime scene. But none of these transient pariahs offered to help. Why would they? They were there for nothing more and nothing less than to have a good time and pick up the latest bit of trade.

Jumping into a taxi, we were at the Infirmary's accident and emergency department within minutes. Dependent on how you viewed the world, it was either very lucky or very unfortunate that Carla was on duty that evening. The hairs on the back of my neck stood up as the whites of our eyes met. Nether the less, she was an excellent nurse and soon made a thorough assessment of the extent of my man's injuries. The stark white examination light left nothing to the imagination. His face was dripping in blood. Both eyes were so oedematous that he couldn't open them. I am sure that I spotted the imprint of a signet ring cut into his temple. Carla gently bathed his wounds and applied steri strips to the gaping lacerations that covered his face. He could hardly speak through his swollen lips. We were whisked into the next available cubicle and waited to be seen by a medic. Dr Stokes appeared from behind the screen, instantly casting a shadow of hope as he went to work. You could tell that he cared and was a sensitive chap under his rugged charm and long black curls. Danni looked uncomfortable, making very little eye contact or effort to chit-chat with him. I wasn't sure if this was worry or if there was more going on behind the scenes. However, this was not the time and place to ask her. Following his examination, Dr Stokes developed a plan and a CT head scan was ordered.

On our way out of the triage room, Carla grabbed hold of my hand and spoke for the first time since she had snubbed me.

"Max, I don't know what to say to you. I am so sorry for my behaviour. I don't know what came over me. I have had a lot going on, but there is no excuse for how I treated you. I was shocked, scared, and frightened."

Hesitating for a second, I thought of all the things that I could have said. I was dying to tell her that I still craved the person I thought she was. For Christ's sake, she had even given me a fob watch. Again, this was not the time or place. Was it kindness or cowardness, who knows? I just knew that I was done with her. Jack was my priority. I simply replied,

"You and me both Carla, you and me both," as I turned away on my blood-soaked heal to follow my friends into the CT Scanner.

I wasn't sure if it was due to his shock, hurt, copious amount of cheap lager or his head trauma. However, Jack was not forthcoming surrounding his injuries and remained evasive when interviewed. He told Dr Stokes that he wasn't entirely sure of how he had sustained the blow or who had hit him. Luckily, there was no physical damage that couldn't be remedied with a couple of dressings and paracetamol. With a clear head scan and bloodwork, he was diagnosed with a concussion. He was advised to come back if there were signs of neurological changes. Danni and I planned to watch over him for the next twenty-four hours at least, anyway. Paul was missing. When he rose the next morning, it was time to tackle him,

"What the hell has been going on here Jack? " Danni demanded.

He knew that he was cornered and finally winced the truth out, resting his head on my chest and blubbering uncontrollably. Myrtle was as comfortable with spreading salacious gossip as he was taking advantage of young gay men. He was no stranger to a nameless fuck in the stench of a urine-soaked cottage, either. As if bursting to announce the winner to an Oscar nominee, he exposed Paul's eagerness to drop to his knees and blow him in a cubicle. Paul was humiliated and unable to control his anger for a minute longer. He had just enough time to take it out on Jack for one last time before he stormed off into the night. Jack slowly lifted his T-shirt to display his history of abuse. Some bruises were fading, but many were as fresh and raw as the blood that ran down his face. Paul was convinced that Jack and I were sleeping together, forcing him into having an HIV test when he found out about Daniel. It now made perfect sense why the Woman's Weekly was such an interesting read. I couldn't get my head around all of this. Why didn't he tell us?

Chapter Ten

I wasn't sure it was such a good idea when Jack mentioned it, but he wanted to escape for a while. And who was I to deny him anything after all he had done for me? Whilst not exactly Las Vegas, if you squinted your eyes tightly enough, the donkeys on the beach could pass for the many ancient cocktail waiters that traipsed the same route of the more salubrious casinos. But just like Vegas, the allure of cheap booze, sweaty bodies and endless opportunities for senseless sin was just too much of a pull. Our B and B was located to fall onto the street and into the nearest gay club. Wryly smiling as we lay on the double bed together, I imagined all the comings and goings that the mattress had seen over the years. Its natural sag willed us together. Try as we might, any moments of tenderness were drowned by our giggles. It creaked beneath us like a rusty tin man, devoid of lubrication. Maybe I was rusty too!

But the mattress did have its way with us. A spark of something new flamed between us and our groins met. I could feel him on my lips. Clutching his hard buttocks, I pulled him onto me. I wanted him so badly as I inhaled his hot sweat. We writhed like two rattlesnakes, groaning and panting. I dug my nails into his shoulders and felt him get harder and harder. Oh, God, what was happening? His firm thighs rubbed against me. He was wet and fucking beautiful. In a split second, our lives could change forever. But for once, I listened to my brain rather than my dick. And then slid from under him and stopped before it was too late. A few minutes later and now in control, we chatted.

"Jack, I love you with every ounce of my soul, I do. I am completely torn, as I want you so badly. But the timing is wrong for both of us. If we come together, it should be for the right reasons. We need to work through our own shit first. I love you and I don't want to ruin that for a moment of pleasure. Please don't let this come between us. I just love you too much to lose you," I panted nervously, with remnants of the sweet flavour of his skin still on my tongue.

Covering us both up in the duvet, he replied, "Yes, I know, you are right Max. We are both two broken souls wandering through a sea of pain trying to anchor ourselves onto some stability."

"Well, that sounds a bit dramatic Jack, even for you, I wouldn't have gone that far. However, I will say, now I understand how you have got your nickname."

We burst into tears of laughter. And just like that, order between us was restored. We put it down to the Blackpool effect. It was a place like nowhere on earth where anything could occur. And as they say, what happens in Blackpool stays in Blackpool.

Later in the evening, we were drunk as monkeys and danced the night away at the Flamingo gay club. Maybe a more accurate name would be the Tarantula as this web dripped in hedonistic hot pleasure. It was our four-floor temple to everything that we needed. Jack was the Alexis Colby to my Crystal Carrington as we scoured the dance floor, secretly rating the local talent as if we were judges at the Eurovision Song Contest. We shamelessly hunted for a '...and our ten points go to' man. Yes, we were drunk but certainly not desperate. Neither would be settling for a 'Luxemburg- Nil poi'. Trying to balance and eat a doner kebab and chips on the way back whilst holding each other in a vertical position was an art form in itself. Lettuce and pizza bread trailed behind us as we staggered back to our bed for the night. Covered in chip grease, we collapsed fully dressed and passed out together.

Danni was waiting for us when we got home. I couldn't look at Jack for fear of laughing when she asked if we had sorted our heads out. Raising my eyebrows like an extra in Carry On Nursing I replied,

"Well Danni, what can I say? It depends upon how you view the world."

My timing couldn't have been any worse. If anything, this only stoked her. Her blonde short spikes were as deadly as a sniper's silent pistol as she exploded and ranted at us. But she was just as angry with herself for not spotting what was going on right under her nose. And now she had spent the last two days blaming herself for everything whilst Jack and I had left her high and dry.

"I don't even know about your HIV status, Jack. Paul forced you to have a test, but you never told us the results. And you went through all of that crap alone. You even went to the clinic with Max. How did you sit in that clinic with him? It's a bloody good job that the staff are bound by confidentiality, isn't it? And then you both decided to go and dance the night away in some godforsaken nightclub and do God only knows what to God knows who, whilst I have been sitting here, holding the fort as usual, worried sick about the pair of you. How could I have been so stupid? I teach student nurses communication skills, for Christ's sake. That bastard Paul, had me completely fooled."

Danni was right. Our own Anna Madrigal was seriously pissed off.

"That's it. Let's go to the Potters' arms. We aren't working tomorrow and in my experience, everything looks better after a few pints," I suggested.

And it did. We sat around our usual table with the wonky leg. Jack stared at the floor, ripping a soggy beer mat to smithereens. Following three rounds, he said that his HIV test was negative. He had always practised safe sex. I could vouch for that. Durex makes condoms in extra-large after all. He shook his head and quietly explained,

"I preferred a beating to Paul's demand for bare backing. As much as he tried, he wasn't strong enough to hold me down. I suppose there are some advantages to being built like a brick shit house. And Max, I know that it is sad, but helping you distracted me from my own crap so don't feel guilty."

"I don't feel guilty. I just never realised that you were putting up with so much shit of your own."

Sometimes the truth is all that is needed to press the reset button. It had been decided over the fifth round of drinks that Jack was moving in with Danni as it was still a hop, skip and a jump from her home to the Infirmary. Whilst channelling his inner pantomime dame, Jack announced that he couldn't move in with me, even if I begged him to. Belly laughing whilst clutching his forehead in angst, he screamed that he simply couldn't cope with my Hyacinth Bouquet attention to home detail. He was not going to spend his life polishing my prize wrought iron candlesticks for man or beast. To be honest, he did have a point. I knew that I was excessively house-proud. No one liked a perfectly plumped sofa cushion or the smell of a brightly bleached kitchen more than me. I loved my little own home in respectable street spending many a happy hour keeping up appearances. I had even invested in the kind of thick rose-coloured carpet that you could write your name in. Nothing made me happier than wandering around homeware buying treasures to fill my very own pink palace.

I had pulled off the performance of my life at the bank. It was even worth butching it up like some sort of professional drag king when I lied and signed on the dotted line. Mrs Maria Taylor was a black-haired powerhouse in her forties. I imagined that she was quite a catch in her

HOW CAN WE BE WRONG?

earlier days. But now, her poorly cut navy suit did nothing to hide her ample frame. Unfortunately, her enormous shoulder pads made her look like an American quarterback, rather than the first female bank manager in the local area. With hard work but no fashion sense, she had conquered this male-dominated world. Well, labels were for clothes anyway, regardless of how badly they fitted. On the surface, the bank may have appeared to be progressive, but deep down, it was as conservative as the picture of Margaret Thatcher that hung on the wall behind her. The bank wasn't exactly in the business of giving mortgages to gay people. Especially ones who had an HIV test; regardless of the results. According to our lady prime minister's teaching, gay people were just a poor investment risk; in every sense of the word.

Chapter Eleven

A sister's office is the epicentre of any ward. These penny dreadfuls fill nursing teams with morbid curiosity. But Sharon's office was different. A pin-up of the English rugby team proudly framed her untidy desk. Catching my smirk, she said,

"Please don't worry, my love, when we have finished with you, you will be brilliant. I know that you have already had a few bumps but I believe in you, Max. I wouldn't have offered you the job otherwise."

Following this pep talk, I sprang from her office and into my first day as a staff nurse, greeted by my new nursing family. During my career, I was no stranger to strong women. However, I had never met a Sue before. Sue may have looked like Patsy from *Ab Fab*, but in reality, she was anything but. From her tight blond back combed hair and pink lipstick, her mission in life was to whip me into shape. Like a dose of salts, she went through my documentation and standards of care. She even went out of her way to gain feedback from patients and the nursing team. She dragged me kicking and screaming like a terrible two-year-old having a tantrum. I couldn't even hide behind my usual smile and charm. She had seen it all before and wasn't taking any prisoners. It was time to grow a pair and become a staff nurse.

On Christmas Day morning, we admitted a lady who was critically ill, but her history was ambiguous. She had been found unconscious by the side of a road. A head scan had tragically diagnosed her with a large, inoperable tumour. The pressure of the tumour had caused swelling and midline shift. This poor lady was at imminent risk of cerebral herniation, or coning. In essence, this is a life-and-death condition where the brain is forced through the back of the patient's skull bone. The police were frantically trying to locate her next of kin.

Against a backdrop of tinsel, the team decided to make her comfortable since surgery was just too risky. Usually, no matter how unconscious a person is, staff gently talk to them. But we knew nothing about this lady. What was her name? Where did she live? Was she married? Did she have children? Catching the sound of the radio, I gently sang along to *Silent Night* under my breath and stroked her forehead as the last verse of the carol carried her from this world to the next. I had no idea that Sue had been watching me until I felt her hand on my shoulder.

We received a message that the lady's husband and two young boys were on their way. The police warned us that they were oblivious to the horror waiting for them. I just wanted to help and be part of it. The doors swung open to a stocky man with whiskey on his breath, still wearing his slippers. Two small boys hid their auburn hair in his padded jacket. Sue took the bewildered man into the office with a policeman whilst I did my best to occupy these petrified mites. They were dressed in matching tartan pyjamas beneath blue duffle coats. I smelled shampoo and fabric conditioner as they shook each side of me on harsh plastic chairs. How could I stop them? They wanted their dad and not some poor substitute.

'Mummy not dead, no Mummy not dead' rang over and over again from the youngest boy. The eldest boy shrieked and then collapsed to the floor. How do you tell your children that their mum is dead? Dad asked his boys if they would like to have the opportunity to say goodbye to her. No matter how traumatic, he believed that 'seeing was believing'. Sue and I followed the family into the side room. They were reunited with their blue-lipped mother for one last time. Both boys told their mummy how much they loved her. They wailed uncontrollably, but at least had the chance to say goodbye. Sue and I did our best to catch them as they fell. Dad told his boys that Mummy was safe in heaven and they would see her again, but not for a very long time. And it was Ok to cry with them too.

My hands were shaking as I gripped the sides of the steaming hot tea cup. Sue smiled and gently explained,

"Max, this is why we do what we do. It's really difficult at times, I can't sugar coat it for you. We are there for people through thick and thin. I saw you for the first time today and you didn't try to hide."

Her sharp features softened as we chatted. I could feel far more than just the warmth from the drink. It was these connections that silently formed the relationships with my nursing family.

But like in many families, it wasn't all drama and stress. There was fun to be had behind the drip stands and bedpans. Sally Bucket was the affectionate nickname for one of the care support workers in our merry band. She was famous for putting on her heirs and graces and spinning her tongue-in-cheek stories of being part of the upper crust. Within her Victorian pile, she had a whole host of serving wenches. In reality, we all knew that Sally and her long-suffering, hen-pecked husband had been renovating a dilapidated Victorian house. She was the devil incarnate with a blonde bob, and we got up to all sorts of mischief together. She was the Laurel to my Hardy, the Morcombe to my Wise and the Cissy to my Ada.

"Well, do you think that Sister Jackie will like her gift when she arrives for duty in the morning?"

As if loitering to marvel at a piece within the Tate Modern, she replied,

"What's not to like about an old pair of man's white fronts with a dirty stain on the back? Every girl would love it. Were you a *Blue Peter* fan? The way you have attached that penis to the pants is a thing of beauty. And you are so resourceful too. Who would have thought that a pink plastic bag, toilet paper and Sellotape could be fashioned in such magnificence? You have even managed to make realistic pubic hair with that sliced cardboard urinal. To my reckoning, you must have seen a few in your time to be so accurate. You are wasted as a staff nurse Max, you really are."

And Sister Jackie truly did love her gift. The very next morning she raced up the ward wearing my creation for the world to see.

Without even trying, I was becoming a millionaire. I arrived home to find a large plastic agency sign attached to the outside of my house. There were already a few messages flashing on the phone from the neuroscience team, including Sister Sharron, asking for extra shifts. And then I clicked that Sally's renovations had started life as a nursing agency.

But she wasn't the only curiosity in our team. There was Dangerous Denise, a nurse who meant well but was aptly named as she was always on the verge of accidentally killing someone. She worked with her trusty sidekick, Bionic Brenda who was anything but. I was particularly fascinated by a slender grey-haired wisp of a creature in her early fifties. Bernadette was a bible-thumping, born-again Christian. She had turned to God for salvation. Rumour had it that she had done favours for sailors in a previous existence. Who was I to judge, anyway? Luckily for her, the only bending she had to do these days was when providing patient care. She hated it if anyone blasphemed and shook her swear box at you in disgust.

I was staggering home after a very busy night shift, trying to mind my own business. My black cotton sheets were calling me by my name.

And there was no cum soaked peach involved either. What the bloody hell was that? Who was trying to kill me? That pea-green Skoda had only missed me by a gnat's pube. A frenetic silhouette on the other side of the steamy windscreen was now trying to grab my attention. As I stormed over to give the driver a piece of my mind, it was like watching the home screen of dial-up internet come into focus as his window slowly came down. And then the near murderer revealed himself in pixelated perfection. My anger fell away as easily as a pair of silk boxers. Finally materialised in full technicolour glory, he was an instant tonic for my sore eyes.

"Is that you Max? I thought that you were drunk. I didn't realise it was you at first, but I noticed a male nurse staggering down the pavement, carefully trying not to fall on the ice. At this time in the morning especially, I was concerned. I'm just on my way to work at the Mortuary and wanted to make sure that you are Ok. I haven't seen you in years. I'm sorry. I didn't mean to startle you. Get in, let me take you home please, you look as if you are about to fall over, you poor thing, you must have had a busy shift, I've got time to drop you off before I start. My patients won't mind waiting a little longer."

Without thinking, I got into his death trap and tried my best to make small talk as we lunged towards my house. I had completed my stint of night shifts and now had a few days off to recover.

"That is very good news for me, Max. Now that I know where you live, can I call in to say hello properly on my way home from work tonight? By then you will have had a chance to catch up on your beauty sleep, not that you need it. How does seven sound?"

With the smell of his Armani aftershave still under my nose, he sped off into the morning sun before I could say no. Was Wayne flirting or just being friendly? It was just too much to think about now.

My heavy eyes landed on the digital clock. Shit, it was now seven o'clock. Where had the last ten hours gone? With the grace of a newborn donkey, I flung on my dressing gown and catapulted towards the door, catching hold of my dishevelled reflection in the mirror in disgust. And there he was, standing in the dark and still knocking. He was smirking like the cat who had just got the cream.

Instead of requesting an audience with Max, he disappeared into my kitchen and returned a few minutes later, placing a hot cup of tea gently into my hands. This was a strange move to make, but I liked it. Whilst I slowly gathered my thoughts together, he sat quietly beside me on my prized Aztec print sofa. Wayne knew how to make good tea. By my third mug, I was able to string a coherent sentence together without sounding like Bag Puss on Temazepam.

"Right, Max, you look like you've not eaten in days. I know it is odd, but can I cook for us both? I'm a dab hand with an all-day breakfast."

"Er, yes, if you want to, but..."

And without letting me finish, he disappeared into the kitchen. I heard him rattling around in my cupboards, frantically hunting for buried treasure. But I wasn't Fanny Craddock by any stretch of the imagination. My fridge was usually stocked with beer rather than food. To be honest, it was just a glorified extension of the off licence.

"Right, I'm just popping out to the late shop to get us a few essentials. You can't make an omelette without breaking an egg."

As soon as his tank trundled from my perfectly manicured block paving, I jumped under the shower and chucked my jeans and a fresh shirt. As he eyed me from top to bottom when the door opened, he sniggered,

"Max, where do you keep your portrait? Is your middle name Dorian?"

"How rude. Get on and make my breakfast if that is what you are going to do? I'll have another cup of strong hot tea too?"

"Is that how you like your men?"

"What do you mean? Hot, strong, or just rude?" I laughed.

He was hell-bent on cooking and forced my poor kitchen into life with a medley of bacon, sausage, and fried eggs, served with a side helping of humour. Wayne chopped mushrooms with surgical precision. Such a handy skill to have in his line of work. My mind wandered to our chance meeting in the mortuary changing room. I had seen him glisten in nothing more than a hospital towel. If anything, he had become buffer over the last few years. He reminded me of a young Elvis Presley. For the first time since moving in, my house smelt like home.

We sat at my circular pine table and I lit one of my candle sticks in honour of the occasion. He proudly carried his feast without dropping a single morsel upon my deep pile. That would be a fate worse than death. His food greased the conversation between us. I developed a really bad case of verbal diarrhoea and just couldn't shut up.

"Wayne, I am ashamed of myself. Nameless sex doesn't numb the pain. But that hasn't stopped me. Grope, pant, sweat, release and then disgust. I never say no. I can't tell Danni, she would kill me. It would rip Jack's heart out, too. But a quick fuck in the bushes is all I am good for."

"Max, we all have secrets. That doesn't make you a bad person, you are allowed to make mistakes. But you don't have to tell everyone, everything either."

"They have been so good to me Wayne, they are better than my birth family"

"Yes, I get that, but what are you going to achieve by telling them? It's only the truth if it won't hurt them. You have told me, I understand. Daniel has played with your head. But that doesn't mean that you need to put an advert in the paper about it. Just chill."

"I'm sorry."

"Don't be, but what do you want out of life, Max?"

No one had asked me that before. I had spent so much time reacting that I had forgotten what I wanted or even needed. Whatever it was, it couldn't be found at the bottom of a glass of whiskey or face down at the Queen's Park.

He focused on my every word. He was a very rare breed; handsome and sensitive. Taking a deep breath, he said,

"Thank you for sharing your honesty with me, Max. You have certainly gone through the wringer. As they say, what doesn't kill you makes you stronger."

"What do you mean, Wayne? I'm all ears. Oh, sorry, it was the wrong thing to say. What I meant was, do you want to talk? I'd love to hear more about you."

Wayne sat snuggled up to the grey-haired, green-tweed-suited man. He was always comforted by Grandad Arthur's blend of old-spice aftershave, tobacco and kindness. They sat for hours together as this tin pot pianist tickled the well-worn ivories to the delight of his inebriated audience. Wayne couldn't hear the music, but that didn't matter to him. He was happy to sit and feel the vibration of the piano as his grandad belted out the ditties to the locals. Like the rest of the pub, the rickety piano stool had seen better days. It kicked and rocked like a pubescent donkey to the pianist's wilful persuasion. He loved it when he felt his grandad sing along to the music. Grandad loved the good old stuff as he put it. This could be anything from George Formby to Frank Sinatra. The well-oiled melodies of *When I'm Cleaning Windows* and *My Way* hung in the air of this working-class boozer like the smoke from a pack of woodbines. He was no Liberace, but still managed to entertain the drinkers. Quite often, a staggering local, full of Dutch courage, joined them at the upright. With equal amounts of exuberance and intoxication, it was commonplace for a wanna-be Shirley Bassey or Tom Jones to slur out a song to the unsuspecting drinkers at The Miner's Retreat.

Grandma Nellie had her sticky own stage that she tirelessly performed from. Against the backdrop of fairy lights and dusty optics, this auburn-haired woman worked her fingers to the bone. Wise words of kindness were administered with each pint she poured. Nellie was more therapist than a voluptuous landlady to the locals. From behind her thick-rimmed glasses and floral prints, she managed to find the right words of comfort. Times were hard and money was tight within this working-class community. As a rule of thumb, people either worked at the local pot banks, the cotton mills or down the coal mines. A drop of liquid relief, a kind word and a sing-song was a welcome diversion to such dusty deprivation.

Wayne loved the pub. The locals affectionately called him the Miner's Retreat boy. It was less spit and sawdust and more coal dust and china clay. There was a function room at the rear of the premises that could be hired out to the local community. Nellie and Arthur were experts at providing hospitality on a shoestring. There was always a steady trade of shotgun wedding receptions and funeral wakes to cater for. Nellie's crusty spam baps, cheese and pineapple on cocktail sticks and savoury oatcakes were welcomed at both events. The only difference was the colour of table cloths. Without this definition, it was hard to judge which was which as both inevitably degenerated into caustic tears of regret. Against the chipped red anaglypta walls and green leatherette chairs of the function room, Nellie and Arthur served exactly what was needed at the time. If it was humanly possible, the front bar room was even starker than the function room. This was a real working-class boozer. And as such, practicality over comfort reigned. Nellie made sure that all of the surfaces were wiped clean. If a coal-dusted miner or clay-covered pottery worker coughed up half a lung over the bar whilst taking a drag from a roll-up, then it didn't matter. It could all be sluiced down with the beer dregs. Different generations of drinkers were imprinted into the very mahogany of the tables and chairs. Grandfather, father, and grandson all gravitated towards the same beer pumps. It was just a rite of passage in this close community.

The circular bar interconnected the two rooms. As a rule, visiting children weren't allowed within the pub. Children played outside together on the grass verge whilst their parents their ale. Now and then, they were dished a bottle of pop and a packet of crisps from the outdoor; a serving window from the bar to the outside world. Nellie was their beer-soaked Mary Poppins. Wayne loved playing with the children. Their parents warned them to be kind to the miner's retreat boy. It wasn't his fault that he was deaf and dumb. His mother, Angela, also worked behind the bar. This blonde beauty wore thick mascara and PVC black boots to provide the necessary eye candy as she pulled the pints. She could have given Agnetha Fältskog a run for her money on any day of the week. Tips were always plentiful, with her cleavage bouncing over the bar.

Bang! Life changed. Their eyes were seared in a lethal mist. What was happening? Some sick bastard had thrown a full bag of dry concrete dust through the closed pub window. This caustic mushroom bomb splintered fragmented glass into the very heart of the pub. Coughing and wheezing in agony, silhouettes tried to find the door. Shrieks of agony rang from the people who were closest to the window. Dazed zombies were injured and bleeding. Acid pain had blocked their bearings. Wiping it away just made their skin burn more. Nellie took hold of her blood-covered husband and guided him towards the light. Without his glasses, Arthur couldn't see a thing. Outside of the pub, broken casualties sobbed and spluttered at the realisation of the devastation. They made makeshift bandages and eye shields with ripped shirts. People appeared from their terraced houses to help. Ambulances blurted in the background as the walking wounded waited for care and attention.

But then real pain stunned the injured into silence.

"Wayne, Wayne, Wayne. Wayne has gone? My boy has gone. Help, please, someone please help me. He is not in the pub, he is not outside, where is he? Please, someone, please?".

Angela's boy was missing. Brave cap-wearing men used dirty hankies as makeshift shields and went back inside. They searched through the debris for the Miner's Retreat boy. Angela was held back by her mother as she tried to clamber back inside. It was just too dangerous.

No court restraining order would stop Harry. It was like taking candy from a baby as he snatched the scrawny bastard from the pub. Wayne was finally his to do whatever he wanted whenever he wanted to do it. Unlike his bitch of a mother, the boy couldn't blab. This would teach Angela to keep her fucking fat mouth shut in the future. If only he could strip her naked now. He smiled to himself and remembered the sound of her sobs. Throwing her in that rat-infested coal house overnight was a master stroke.

This lying bitch would be put in her place once and for all. If he couldn't hurt her, then her son would pay. Fashioning himself on a young Elvis Presley, he had fooled everyone into believing that he was great. There was no serenade of '*Love Me Tender*' when the wedding ring was placed upon Angela's finger. She belonged to him now. On their wedding night, he ripped off her white dress and showed her who was boss. What was a bit of blood, anyway? He had done his homework. In the eyes of the law, it didn't count now that they were married. Who did that slut think that she was? She paraded around in that fucking pub as if she owned it.

That heavily pregnant bitch did bounce after all. He stepped over her at the bottom of the stairs and noticed that she was bleeding from below. Well, they weren't his children, anyway. Twins didn't run in his family. The father had to be someone she had fucked at that pub. That is where they met and a Leppard doesn't change its spots. He watched her slide like a blood-smeared slug across the linoleum to the phone. It was just a pity that he didn't have any salt to hand. Her struggle just made it more fun to watch. Leaning over her, he saw that this whore was trembling. Now he needed to cover his tracks before the ambulance arrived. He rasped into her ear he would once kill her if she breathed a word of this to anyone. That should do the trick. Hearing the ambulance crew arrive at the door gave him just enough time to drag her body from the floor and onto the sofa.

Both of his twin sons were born prematurely, but only Wayne survived. Angela's life hung in the balance as the midwives and doctors did their best to resurrect her. On admission to the maternity unit, she existed somewhere between blood-soaked life and death. They were shocked by the extent of this poor woman's injuries. Those stairs must have been so steep when she slipped. The local priest was called and waited in the wings, just in case. This gave Father Alan, a young plump priest, ample time to comfort her husband. He may have been fresh out of seminary school, but the catholic priest recognised shock when he saw it. Father Alan was worried that this cross would be too much for this poor man to bare .

He sat quietly numbed, almost devoid of emotion, whilst Father Alan prayed to God the Father, God the Son and God the Holy Spirit for guidance. *Our Father in Heaven hallowed be your name.* He didn't even appear to flinch at the news of his new-born's death. He just shook his head in pasty silence. *Your Kingdom comes, and you will be done, on earth as you are in heaven.* He was in such a deep state of denial at the news. *Give us this day our daily bread. Forgive us our sins as we forgive those who have sinned against us.* All that the priest could offer was the quiet power of prayer to soothe this man's suffering. Clutching onto the rosary beads in his pocket for reassurance, he continued, *Lead us not into temptation, but deliver us from evil.* Father Alan was only sure of one thing that night. Yes, only the love of the holy spirit could repair the devastation within this beautiful family.

Angela wondered what had happened to her dead son. She never got to see him before he was wrapped in a sheet and whisked away to the dirty sluice for disposal. She was desperate to hold her cold blue boy, kiss him on his blood-soaked head and tell him that she was sorry. All she wanted was a moment with him to say goodbye. Had he had been buried in an unmarked grave? Had he been incinerated with the infirmary's surgical waste? She just hoped that somehow, someday, she would find out what had happened to her baby. Until then, she couldn't grieve for him. No one seemed to understand that having one surviving baby was not a consolation for the death of her other twin. But, nether the less, she loved Wayne and did everything in her power to ensure that he thrived. She force-fed him every hour, on the hour, as the midwife had insisted. Nellie and Arthur were amazing when she returned to the pub with her bundle of bones in a white crocheted shawl. Arthur had cleaned up her old cot. At last, she was home and finally safe.

It took a while for Wayne's eyes to adjust to the dark. They were still hurting from the dust in his eyes. It smelt so dirty down here. He stood shivering with his back against the cold wet wall, hoping that it wouldn't be as bad as last time. That man held his face against the concrete floor and made him bleed inside. Sitting down just hurt too much. But he was lucky. Wayne wasn't on his own here. When the worst of it happened, his friend was always there to hold his hand. It was really strange because he could hear this boy talking to him.

"Just breathe, you are not alone, I am here with you, look at me, it will be all over soon, just keep on looking at me. Don't give up."

Not only could Wayne hear him, but this little boy also looked like him too. It was as if he was staring in a mirror. Wayne found it easier to pretend that he wasn't there when the man hurt him. He tried to imagine himself back in the pub, playing the piano with Grandad Arthur. But even his imagination didn't work sometimes. The pain was just too much. The light hurt his eyes when the policeman opened the cellar door. Wayne didn't know how long he had been down there. He was just glad it was over.

And that is how the child psychologists, the police and social workers became acutely aware that Wayne did not have a learning disability. He was able to vividly explain with dolls, teddy bears, and pictures what had happened to him in that dank hell. There wasn't a dry eye in the house when the professionals reviewed his sketches. At the age of seven, Wayne received speech therapy. At the age of eight, this amazing boy learned how to read.

I was just myself with Wayne and in return, he had opened up to me. Just when I thought that things couldn't get any better, he dropped into our conversation that he was gay. Hallelujah! *Zipididy do da, zippidy day, Oh my world what a wonderful day!* Things were looking up. The more we chatted, the more I began to like him. The honey-coloured candlelight danced around my virgin plaster as if bringing the whole room alive for the first time. I felt warm, well-fed, secure, and understood. After all, Wayne had already seen me at my worse and still decided to come back for more. But I wanted more than casual sex. Look where that had got me in the past. Only a good old-fashioned romance would do. Taking inspiration from my comic heroin, the words of Hattie Jacques popped into my head. Over our candlelit breakfast, I talked about the iconic scene in *Carry on Matron*. Hattie famously fought off Kenneth's misplaced affections with

'I'm a simple woman, with simple tastes. I want to be wooed'.

Like Hattie, I had decided that Kenneth's response of 'You can be as *wude* as you like with me' would not cut the mustard. And to my utter amazement, Wayne was in full agreement. Bingo.

Chapter Twelve

I couldn't wait to see Jack the next day and talk all things Wayne before Danni joined us at the pub. He smirked when I explained the bizarre sequence of events that had unfolded only the day before. What a difference a day makes. I stopped babbling and looked into his eyes for some sort of reassurance at best, or just a reaction at worse. Either way, the next few seconds seemed to last a lifetime. Finally, a glint of wickedness darted from one eye to the other. Cackling like an old witch, he spurted from over the rim of his pint glass,

"Well then, what did his hot salty sausage taste like? Did it fill you up or has it left you gagging for more?"

"He was a perfect gentleman. He may have wined and dined me, but there was no seventy-minus-one, going on. Hold on to your pearls, Jack, but I want to get to know him."

But Jack had news of his own to share with me. Still grinning like the Cheshire cat, he swigged back the last of his pint as if his life depended upon it before slamming it on the table. I took the hint; it was my round. All he wanted to do was to have a little fun. And I didn't blame him either. My tin soldier had been through enough. He had got himself a new job. How had I missed that one? It turned out that he would be moonlighting on the bar of a drag club for a few nights a week. He had apparently smashed his audition with the preciseness of his tambourine shaking. All that military training hadn't been wasted after all. Was there no end to his talents? In a tight white vest and even tighter groin-hugging denim shorts, he was about to grace the 'European Cabaret Bar.' We would have to get him a reinforced jock strap as a matter of urgency. I didn't want some poor punter copping an eye full of something more than what they had bargained for. Some urgent field research was desperately needed. This would mean a trip to the male surgical ward. Sister Dickson was an expert on the intricacies of the male truss. She would probably have a bloody stroke, or even two, if she really liked it. Jack howled as I unveiled my plan.

My big butch friend had gone camp for the summer. I was flummoxed but very happy for him at the same time. But that was not all. Amongst the breastplates and feather boas, he had been seduced by the beaded lashes of one of the star drag queens. By day, Adam was an unassuming shop assistant in a men's clothes shop. But by night, he was transformed into his blonde, six foot tall, alter ego Miss Eclair'. I couldn't wait to go and see Nancy perform her routine on the bar with her handsome tambourine-shaking beau. Only front-row tickets would do for such a spectacle.

Danni joined us around an hour later. Luckily she was no stranger to our drunken banter, and it didn't take her long to catch up with us. I'm sure that girl had hollow legs and a weak gag reflex by the way she knocked back the beer. She belly laughed at our news, hiccupped and slurred.

"The Drag Queen and the Mortician. It sounds like the title for a farce to me, boys. You certainly know how to pick them. Well, as long as you are both happy. That's all that matters to me. Everyone else can do one as far as I am concerned."

Jack was determined to reveal the third new story of the night. He had got to know Danni on a whole new level since the odd couple had been living together. But no, this wasn't just the normal hair in the sink or rim around the bath story. This tale was a real corker. Jack had been picking up mysterious interference on his portable TV at random times in the evening. There was no rhyme or reason for this strange phenomenon. Like a prima ballerina, he pirouetted around the bedroom, waggling his indoor aerial in several positions. Exasperated and confused, he was just about to give up the ghost and collapse on the bed. And then he heard a slow hum that coincided with the nuisance. On close inspection, he discovered that this noise was mysteriously drifting from behind Danni's paper-thin bedroom walls. It took a further few nights for Jack to realise that Danni's vibrator was interfering with the signal to his portable. The shame of it. I thought that I was going to aspirate on my lager.

Tonight, I wanted a torch song quartet. I wasn't in the mood to settle for a trilogy. It was time to address the pink elephant in the room once and for all. Danni was quite cagy about her love life and skilled in deflecting any direct questions over the years. This was getting on my nerves since she practically knew my inside leg measurement. Drumming up the Dutch courage, I had stopped her in her tracks.

"Ok, ok, it's not fair, is it, boys? It's time to come clean. You both deserve to know the truth. I'm sorry, it's only right. Well, it's like this. You know that cruel joke that some doctors use between them to insult us, nurses don't you... 'what's the difference between a nurse and a toilet...a toilet doesn't follow you around for months afterwards when you shit on it.' Sadly, in my case, it's no laughing matter. It ended when you both swanned off to Blackpool for the weekend. That probably explains my outburst now, doesn't it? Transference is a wonderful thing."

Passion just knows no boundaries. Her affair with Dr John Stokes, the consultant over the male surgical ward, had been going on for a couple of years. He was the same dashing doctor who had patched

Jack up in the accident and emergency department. She knew deep down that he would never leave his wife. By then, it was too late; she was head over heels in love with him. John only married his wife out of obligation. She used the oldest trick in the book to snare him by saying that she was pregnant. As a traditionalist by nature, he stuck by her. Equally, he didn't want to lose face or his father's financial support. So that was that, he 'did the right thing' and married her. Eventually, a baby did appear two years later.

John was in pieces when he phoned her. Danni was like a moth to the flame when it came to him. She had absolutely no choice but to meet him when he phoned her and told her the news. Baby Stokes had been put at risk. Daniel was his wife's midwife. All they did know for certain was that Daniel may have put the entire family at risk. And now they would all be tested for HIV, including his newborn son. John shook in fear as Danni wiped the tears from his cheeks. She still loved him. He smelt so good as he held her in his arms. The mixture of salt, patchouli and desperation was intoxicating. He kissed her gently on both cheeks as he unbuttoned his starched white coat. She leaned into his firm body and feverishly stroked the bedraggled mop of black hair that hung over his face. He towered over her in heated anguish. There was something so beautiful about him. In the heat of the moment, sensibility and restraint went through the window.

The clatter of a cleaning trolley interrupted their embrace as it lunged into the linen cupboard. But Bren just smiled and reassured them that their secret was safe with her. She was all too familiar with the devastating effects of the hospital grapevine. It was an unseen silent poison that crept through the very heart of the City Infirmary. Regaining her composure, Danni mopped her forehead with one of the pillowcases, zipped up her dress, re-arranged her parrots, and left

John in the laundry room without looking back. Now it was finally over.

Danni watched as her blood was sucked into the unwelcoming syringe. She felt like a leper when the phlebotomist double-wrapped the sample within a further biohazard bottle. She shook her head in acknowledgement of the at risk of infection warning label. Mrs Thatcher had it wrong, HIV was not reserved for the gay community and intravenous drug users. Daniel had delivered Baby Stokes and she had been sleeping with his father. The ripple effects were far-reaching. She felt dirty and stupid all at the same time, kicking herself for not having the strength to end her relationship with John sooner. And now she was being punished for loving a man who was never hers to keep. In silence she waited out the next two weeks for her test results to become available, wondering if she was going to live or die. Getting a negative test result only confirmed one thing. It was finally over with Dr John Stokes. There was just the need for one more phone call between them before she sent him off for his life of respectability. She could hear his sobs echoing down the telephone as they said their goodbyes. At the same time, she was relieved to hear that he and his family were all HIV-negative.

Within the click of a finger, I was sober again. Danni just couldn't tell anyone, or the cover would have blown on the whole diabolical thing. Trying to find the funny side, she said,

"What a tangled web we weave, eh? Can you imagine what Sister Dickson would say if she knew? She is as austere as the statue of Queen Victoria in the park. I think that bronze is warmer. That ward is her life, she would never recover from the shock! She holds her consultant, Dr Stokes on such a high pedestal. Over the years I have watched her maintain the status quo at all costs. Who am I to bring her calculated empire to its knees? I can practically feel the needles of her voodoo doll in my back as it is."

Skilfully diverting the conversation, Jack decided to educate our bruised rose in antics of my 'rude awakening with Wayne' as he put it. She shook with laughter as he mimicked me running down the stairs like Quasimodo looking for his Esmerelda. Raising her eyebrows over her red rims, she said that she was very familiar with the delights that 'Wayne the Mortician' offered the casual onlooker. She had chatted to him a few times when escorting the newly deceased to the chapel of rest. This fine specimen of manhood was wasted in an environment where there were seldom few to admire him. I couldn't agree with her more. And then it was time for another round of drinks. There had been far too much drama served over the beer than even I could cope with.

Chapter Thirteen

I had found my spiritual home. Anyone could be anything or do anyone within this sticky den of diversity. No one gave a damn if you were black, white, brown, pink or green, had sky blue spots, two heads or seven legs. All were equally welcome at the European as long as you had the money to buy a round or two. As we entered into a real-life version of *La Cage aux Follies*, I expected to see the wonderful Zaza swish past. This melting pot was located right at the edge of the red-light district. People cued for ages to gain entrance and lose their inhibition within the safety of this club. But, as VIPs, we sashayed past them. Being best friends with the act did have its perks. Eccentric couples always punctuated the scene. Within these glossy red walls, I could be myself. It was bad and beautiful, bawdy and bizarre. Themed upon a faded theatre, it was rather gaudy, but also rather grand. The gold tassels of the red heavy velvet drapes danced in expectation as the scrummage moved closer to the bar, wanting to be sure of the best view.

Clutching onto Danni and Wayne for sheer life, I trembled as the lights went down. A few bars of Harvey Fierstein's *I am What I Am* cracked over the sound system. The excitement was too much to bear, well, nearly. A spotlight shone to punctuate a solitary silhouette, standing statuesque with one arm in the air. This slender beauty was wearing a Princess Di-inspired wedding dress, six-inch silver heels, and a long blonde wig. She carried a rather large, netted handbag, filled with fake foam bricks. Miss Nancy Eclair' sprang into action and gave the performance of her life, entertaining her fans with a routine based upon Yvonne Fair's, *It Should Have Been Me*. *I saw my love walking down the aisle, and as he passed me by, he turned and smiled.* She hit Jack several times with her handbag as the lyrics unfolded. *You made a promise that we would never part. And then you turned around and broke my heart.* A mirage of white sequins and lace catapulted from the bar and into the audience. *Now you are standing there saying 'I do,' holding hands with somebody new. It should have been me!* It wasn't our fault that she was with child, looking like she needed a midwife at any given minute and had been rejected by her lover. *Then the preacher asked, 'Will there be silence, please? If any objections to this wedding, speak now or forever hold your peace'.* Jack was genuinely happy for the first time in ages and had such a dab hand with a tambourine, too. I just didn't realise that his therapy would come in the form of a six-foot pregnant drag queen. And now it was my turn to be the butt of her jokes. Nancy winked at me through her beaded lashes, grabbed hold of my shoulders, and shook me into submission. She then dropped to the floor and refused to move. *It should have been me. You know it should have been me, darling. How could you do this to me?* She blamed me for absolutely everything, just managing to wallop me again before the song came to its comic crescendo. *You know it should have been me! I've always been faithful and true!* Miss Nancy then traipsed off, crying to her dressing room as the audience roared for more. Her comic genius was so different to Adam's gentle soul. I guess we all hide behind something. For some, it's a wig and heels whereas for others it's a nurse's uniform. The words of the well-known spiritual guru, RuPaul, seem to make sense now, 'we are all born naked and the rest is drag'.

Wayne was a perfect gentleman. Nothing bad was going to happen to me when he was around. He was patient with my insecurities and did 'court' me in every sense of the word. He made me feel like a king. But there were no over-inflated gestures of grandeur, that just wasn't his style. He showed me how he felt with simple thoughtful actions. Quite often, I would open my lunch box to find a little love letter sneaked in between the sandwich bread. We were just happy to sit quietly together, holding hands as we watched *Coronation Street*. I never felt as if I needed to fill the room with words. With Wayne, it all just felt as natural as breathing. Even my work colleagues noticed my contentment. Wayne delivered us food when I was on night shifts. He giggled in delight at Sally Bucket's delusional ideation. He was always on hand to make one of them a cup of tea and provide some solace after work too. Some of my work family called in to see us both after a busy shift. After all, our home was on the main road to the Infirmary.

And just like that, she had done it again. There was a place for me amongst this old lady's Victorian finery, after all. But this time, it wasn't forced, grand or dramatic. It was just slipping me on like a good girdle. And I was more than happy to hold her up. It was a marriage made in heaven, but like many relationships, it was complicated. Sometimes you have to go through dark times to realise that you are better together. I had never imagined that I would qualify as a nurse, let alone get a job. And here I sat with two years of experience, a teaching qualification under my belt and training as a person-centred counsellor, wondering what Sharron Varley wanted with me now. Once she had finished applying her new shade of red lipstick, she turned to me and said,

"Well Max, when you have finished burning a hole in my calendar, I have some very interesting news for you. As you are aware, Sue has been successful in gaining the post of my latest Junior Sister. She will be working alongside Jackie to support me as we expand our service. We are going to open up a high-dependency unit for our neuroscience patients. This has created a vacancy. We will be advertising for Sue's old job shortly. I wanted you to hear it from the horse's mouth. We think that you are ready to apply for it. It won't be a wasted application if you give it a shot. We will support you to complete the specialist diploma in neuroscience nursing. Now if you would like a closer look at Mr October, I will move my head."

I wasn't staring at her rugby calendar, though. I was trying to make sense of the words that were landing upon me. She certainly had a knack for knocking the wind out of my sails. Had I got the experience to be the next Sue? I didn't see one coming.

I spent less time on my appearance and more time preparing for the anticipated questions themselves. Of course, Danni, as always, was my candle in the wind. She guided me through the National Health Service policy and the rudiments of the local nursing strategy. On the day of the interview, I knew that I was as ready as I would ever be and after a quick shower and throwing my suit on, we headed out. Wayne drove me up to the ward, in what remained of his Skoda. Like a stroppy teenager, it roared 'make me' with every gear change. If this beast could not be tamed, then perhaps it was time for it to retire from service.

In the teachings of Maya Angelou, I took everyone with me who had ever been kind. I carefully tucked them all gently into my breast pocket. I took all the ward team, Wayne, Danni, Jack, Adam in his heels, Aunt Bren smelling of cheap perfume, Mrs M with her pursed lips, Tracey in her pig slippers, Kev and many of the kind people who had shaped my career. There was no place here for Daniel or Carla or any of the traditionists who had tried to knife me. I held my head up high and walked into the interview room to be greeted by Sharron, Jackie, and Sue. I gently lowered myself into the chair. There was no hiding from this panel. They bombarded me like quiz masters from all directions with a series of quick-fired professional, leadership, and clinical questions. And to my amazement, I knew most of the answers. I didn't need to ask the audience or to phone a friend. I still had all of my lifelines intact when the interview finished. The people in my pocket had prepared me well. At the end of the formal questions, the panel momentarily cracked their poker faces as a hint of acknowledgement flickered between them. In the background, I could hear the comforting song of a floor cleaner swirl past the door as if to serenade and soothe me. It took me back to the days when we played the same melody together.

Following the interview, they asked me to wait outside Sharron's office in the visitor's area. This area was as uninviting as it was harsh. This was something that I was going to change. Further down the corridor, a young short-haired domestic lad was dancing the Argentine tango with a floor cleaner. And then I was invited back into Sharron's office. I had done it. The panel could see that I meant every word that I had said. I fell back onto Sharron's desk, making her filing system fly around us like confetti. I almost tripped over the rotatory cleaner's cable as I ran down the ward. But what were Wayne, Danni, Jack and Aunt Bren all doing there? They had been hiding in the patient's dayroom like pensive fathers in a maternity ward. Some of our regular patients were in on the action. Without them, I was nothing. Pip, a young teenager who was living with multiple sclerosis, joined the fun. She wheeled herself towards me at a rate of knots, almost toppling me over like a bowling pin. Life couldn't get any better than this. This was a bag of netted oranges moment if there ever was one. Just like Arnold within the closing scenes of *The Torch Song Trilogy*, I clutched hold of everything important to me, still crying, but extremely grateful.

Chapter Fourteen

Everything about Miss Nancy Éclair fascinated me. I was lucky to be invited backstage on many occasions. The intoxicating odour of hairspray and make-up wafted through the air with the same hypnotic effect as the sweet smell of my former flat's entrance. Her wigs were lovingly manicured as if they had been to a Parisian poodle parlour. There was not one hair out of place as they stared at us like a row of performing pooches. Whilst stuffing foam padding down a pair of industrial-looking tights, she told me that her wigs had been her best friend for many years. Much like these nylons, they had carried her through thick and thin. She smiled as she applied her base layer of foundation. Then, like a proud mother, she reeled off their names to me. There was Cher, Shirley, Bette, Tina, and Marylyn, to name but a few. Her all-time favourite child was Dolly, a larger-than-life, blonde curly number.

She shaved her chest hair, strapped on a breastplate, and explained that her dresses had been closer to her than her own family. That wasn't hard to do since she spent the majority of her teenage years living in the YMCA, before finding her feet in three-inch stilettos. With no money to buy her costumes, she taught herself how to sew and hot glue every sequin until her hands bled. Nancy was a delicate but determined phoenix in star-studded tit tape. And she got my seal of approval when it came to Jack. Behind all the glamour and illusion, Adam was one of the kindest people I had ever met.

My new job was perfect, even if it was difficult to step into Sue's slingbacks. Besides my day job, I also set up a counselling service for patients and their families too. I am an advocate for the absolute necessity of good mental health support to promote well-being. There is no shame in asking for help. Without this help, I doubt that I would have learnt to live and move on from all the trauma related to planet Daniel. There is always someone there, twenty-four hours a day, three hundred and sixty-five days a year. Professional support is only a phone call away.

Wayne and I were as solid as a rock. He had even caught the nursing bug and had landed a job as a health care assistant in a male medical ward a few corridors away from me. Like water off a duck's back, he simply shrugged off the comments by some of the nurses who asked him,

"What's a good-looking man like you doing with Max? Don't throw your life away on him. Did you know that he is riddled with aids?'

On getting wind of these comments, Aunt Bren seemed to be spending a lot more time with Wayne when he was on duty. Quite often she appeared from nowhere, tapping her foot and glaring at the staff. No one would mess with her if they valued their life. It just made me realise how safe and secure I was in the protective bubble of my neuroscience family. They never asked me about my past, judged me or passed comments.

The ward phone rang in a new trauma during one Saturday night shift. We all jumped to alert and prepared for a critically ill patient to arrive at our newly opened high-dependency unit. As if by magic, Sally Bucket sprang into action and started to prepare the bed space.

The patient had already been intubated whilst in the Accident and Emergency Unit and would be prepared for theatre immediately upon arrival to us. He had sustained a traumatic bleed to his head. His aneurysm needed to be clipped within our emergency neuroscience theatre by our extremely knowledgeable and skilled neurosurgeons. The neurosurgeons are one of the most unassuming, earnest and supportive teams of doctors that I have ever had the pleasure of working with. They gently dance around the inside of the patients' skulls with elegance and beauty. It is a true spectacle to see a patient's brain pulsate full of memories and personality within the hands of these gentle saviours. It is the closest thing to heaven that I have ever witnessed. I could not see our patient from the distance of the ward doors as he was cloaked like Medusa in the usual tangle of drips and drains. The beeps of the medical equipment and ventilator played a medical aria as we poised ourselves, ready to receive him.

Not having had the time to change before leaving the European, Miss Nancy Éclair clattered in behind the procession, still clutching Dolly. She was ruined but Nancy really didn't care, wigs could be replaced. Her fringed cowgirl dress was splattered and ripped. Now closer, I saw mascara dripping down her breastplate. And then my legs went weak. A cheese and onion sandwich regurgitated like toxic waste in my mouth. No, it must be a nightmare, but it wasn't. Jack had lost his footing and slipped off the wet bar during the closing number of *Islands in the Stream*. His head cracked on a beer pump before he collapsed into deep unconsciousness.

It was payback time. Without thinking, I jumped into action to help him. I was going to be there for him, right or wrong, whether he was unconscious or awake. I found it almost impossible to let go of his clammy hand as we wheeled him through the plastic doors to the theatre at the end of the ward. Before handing him over to the theatre team, I whispered in his ear,

"Jack, I love you so much, you big daft lump. Don't leave me. I can't live without you."

For a while, I stood in the airlock between the operating theatre and the ward door, wondering which way to turn. Deep down, I knew that Jack would have wanted me to keep it together and do my best to carry on. On my return, Miss Nancy Eclair had left the building. Instead, I saw Adam in a pair of hospital pyjamas, being carefully cradled in a soft blanket by Sally Bucket. She was carefully helping him to tease away the duct tape from around his head. I watched her tenderly rock with him from side to side as she hugged his blubbering body. In this tragedy, I saw only her compassion. This was real life, good old-fashioned nursing care at its best.

Somehow, the next few hours came and went. We sat Adam in the back lounge and plied him with copious amounts of tea whilst waiting for Wayne and Danni to join the vigil. Within ten minutes they were throwing their arms around me. Dishevelled and distressed but with the voice of experience, Danni piped up,

"Max, what the hell are you doing? For God's sake, get someone else to take over. This is not right. There are professional boundaries. Think of your code of conduct. This is too much. Let me phone Sharron, please?"

"No Danni, don't do that. I have a great team behind me and I need to be busy. I have already called the night manager, and she knows the score. She is sending another nurse from A and E to take over from me. I am not that stupid. Please sit with Adam and Wayne in the back lounge whilst I carry on till the morning. I promise to phone Sharron myself if it gets too much. You more than anyone else should understand my reasons. Just let me be."

"As long as you have organised help, Max. You won't be thinking clearly," she said, appearing a little more pacified.

"Yes, I know, this is why I have sorted it out already. I plan to float about. I have worked too hard to qualify as a nurse to do anything stupid or put anyone at risk. I won't be doing anything more taxing than making cups of tea for you all and folding clean linen. With a bit of luck, they won't send me Carla. That is the last thing that I need now. There must be other nurses down there."

Luckily, it wasn't Carla. It was one of the A and E experienced nurses who had recently done a stint in neurosciences. Every time the ward phone rang, the more I bargained with God. But he did answer my prayers. A few hours later, Jack returned to the ward with his aneurysm successfully clipped, still intubated but alive. Contrary to some fractions in public belief, maybe this miracle was God's way of saying that he loves all of his children. If he doesn't judge, then why should anyone else? He doesn't care whether or not you are a tambourine-shaking sidekick to a drag queen boyfriend. His love is universal. When the unsuspecting early shift arrived, they picked up the baton as I crumbled. Danni took Adam home to properly soak away stage makeup and dry blood and I went home to wail the morning away in Wayne's arms.

Once rested, we all returned to the ward. This fidget of a man now lay so still and vulnerable on the bed. My mind flashed back to the first time that I clapped my eyes on him. I remember him clambering in late into the expectant group of new healthcare recruits and later teasing me over the bed bath debacle of hell. And now here he was, a sanitised patient himself. I tasted hospital soap and talcum powder when I got closer and placed a kiss on his forehead. Sister Sue stared up from her observation chart at the foot of the bed, smiled and put her hand on my shoulder. She was good at doing this. Sometimes words are not needed, anyway. Her perfected pinned blonde beehive complemented her new navy blue uniform.

Sharron joined me as I relaxed in the newly renovated visitor's room. She found my hand that had sunk deep into the cushions of the tan leather sofa. Her wide brown eyes looked blotchy, like she had been crying. She explained that she would have come back to work and taken over. It didn't matter whether it was the middle of the night or not. This wasn't a telling off though, she knew that I had made sure that her ward was safe. Sharron told me that no one is an island and that her door was always open. If you look in any good nursing dictionary and flick to the definition of 'compassionate leadership', only two words are available; 'Sharon Varley'.

Over the period of a few days, Jack improved. Slowly his drips and drains were removed to reveal the man I loved. Beneath the sterility of the hospital gown and, much to our relief, his old personality started to emerge. The surgery had been a great success. Whilst not exactly demonstrating my best bedside manner, I leaned closer to him but was careful to avoid his head wounds. I whispered,

"Well, I am relieved that you are getting better. I certainly know that Adam is too. It was such a good job that it was your brain that needed clipping, as you really don't use it that much. Thank God that you didn't land on your penis. That would be a fate worse than death. Half of the gay scene would declare a day of national mourning if anything happened to that. We don't want you to lose your nickname, do we now?"

He coughed as his eyes twinkled in approval. Over the next couple of weeks, he went from strength to strength. We started to plan for his discharge to Danni's home and develop a rota to look after him whilst he convalesced. I wouldn't be feeding him grapes though, if this is what he thought.

I'm so pleased that Sharon had given me a few days off and that I wasn't around to see it happen. The pulmonary embolism was over in a flash. Not that this offered any comfort. Jack wasn't strong enough to survive. Every time I closed my eyes, I imagined Sue and Sharron jumping onto his chest. I heard the back of his bed removed, his clothes rip and the familiar red resuscitation trolley spring into life. Frenetic hands grappled to save him over the hiss of the oxygen. The manic scream of a defibrillator lunged into action as the lead clinician shouted 'Everyone stand clear'. I even heard the thud of his body jolt back onto the bed. But they couldn't save him. Time of death was called. Staff prepared his body and then lowered it into the empty trolley. The squeak of its wheels carried my brother to the hospital mortuary. How could I live without him?

I missed the roughness of Wayne's Skoda. At least that beast made me feel something. Even feeling travel sick was better than nothing. The smoothness of his new VW made the journey seem shorter. The shadow of the Infirmary's chapel of rest loomed towards us, but we weren't ready to get out of the car. And here he was, laid out on the same oak platform where I had cleaned so many times. It just wasn't right. He was covered in a thick, heavy, cream-padded blanket that was fringed in tasteful purple piping. An intricately embossed golden crucifix was embedded within the centre of the covering. His blue hands with black fingernails had been placed outside of the shroud. His head was carefully propped forward on a slither of a satin pillow. His mop of brown hair was carefully combed back to show his mottled complexion, deep purple lips and surgical wound. Wayne gently advised that it was probably wise to hold his hand but not to venture any further under the cover. But holding onto his icy hand just wasn't enough. I knew Wayne was right, but all I wanted to do was to pick my cold man up and hug him for one last time. Sensing my plans,

Wayne and Danni gently took hold of my hands from both sides. They were right, but sometimes right isn't always right. The melodic hum of the fridges broke the silence. Jack had given his heart to us and had asked for nothing in return. It was difficult to leave him here, but we knew we had to go. Danni and Wayne said their long goodbyes, but I couldn't find anything to say. I kissed his cool forehead and left with the taste of formaldehyde fresh on my lips.

Chapter Fifteen

Jack's parents had disowned him years ago. He made no secret of this. A telephone or two later confirmed that their position had not changed. They didn't want to visit him when he was still alive at the hospital and certainly saw no point in seeing him dead. If anything, they seemed relieved. I couldn't put my finger on it, but I knew his mother's voice from somewhere.

Maria trembled as she slammed down the receiver. Jack's death had opened up all sorts of twisted pain again. She wasn't a bad person, right? If only they knew her truth. Perhaps his friends wouldn't be so quick to judge if they knew what she had been putting up with for all of these years. Memories gnawed to be released from that compartment in her head. The anti-depressants just couldn't keep a lid on her pain for one second later. A searing creak of her arthritic knees signalled her fall to the floor. And there she wailed on her pink oriental rug, wondering which way was up.

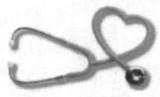

She sat on the bandstand casually wiping her red rocket lolly off her white crochet cardy. Her mother would kill her if this got stained too.

It was no fun when she was grounded. She thought that her mother was going to lose the plot. There was no hiding from those tell-tale grass stains on her Sunday best dress. It didn't take long for her mother to put two and two together and make five. She gently ran her hand over her lips. In her mind's eye, she could still taste that carbolic soap on her breath from last time, when her mother tried to wash her 'dirty mouth' out. But it was a price worth paying for such pleasure. Goodness me, George was insatiable. He was just a horny octopus. And Maria had the love bites to prove it. Luckily, they had been carefully placed in more discreet places where prying eyes could not see. No one could imagine what was going on behind his beautiful blonde locks and innocent blue eyes. She had got pally with him at Sunday school. Now they were discovering far more than the scriptures together. If you listened quietly, you could almost hear Queen Victoria state that 'we are not amused' as she presided over their pubescent passion. Even the sternness of her statuesque frown could not dampen George's harder. There certainly was a lot of feverish fun going on among the fuchsia-filled flower beds. And just like the delicate buds around them, these lovers blossomed with each new bandstand encounter.

Maria was headstrong if nothing else, determined to be more than a housewife, tied to the kitchen sink, warming her husband's slippers by the fire, ready for him to return from work. No, she had a mind of her own and she proved it by excelling in every subject before leaving grammar school. She may have had a passion in her pants for George, but her head was firmly screwed on, too. Taking one last glance in the hall mirror and a final spray of lacquer to her black glossy hair, she headed out to the first day at the bank. Being a cashier was just the first step on her ladder. But for now, Maria just had to learn to walk in her black heels without falling up the three marble steps that led to the bank. She clattered through the brass door with the style and grace of an adolescent hyena. But she didn't care, what the staff thought of her. Her eyes were set on one thing and one thing only. One day, her name would be etched onto the brass plate on the bank manager's door. They wouldn't be laughing then or dare to call her a poor man's Dianna Rigg.

He spun her around the dancefloor like a whirling dervish. Mr and Mrs George and Maria Taylor were officially on show for the whole world to admire. His guiding hand rested on her delicate white embroidered bodice. Her rhinestone tiara shimmered like ice in the ballroom lights whilst holding her netted veil in place. The rough crinkle of her underskirts swished past her thigh as they navigated the dancefloor. *Maria* from *West Side Story* echoed around the banqueting hall. George never left the passions of the bandstand without blurting out a few lines of these lyrics to her. With exacting attention to detail, her beloved fuchsias took centre stage in the table displays. They were even featured in her bride's bouquet that she had only tossed a few short hours ago. There was not a dry eye in the house as the wedding party watched the first-ever female bank manager and her dashing blonde oncologist in a grey morning suit waltz around the ballroom floor. The couple were over the moon to hold their wedding in the gothic hall at the local University Campus. Whilst the upper crust was long gone, it seemed only fitting for such a well-regarded couple. After all, this wedding did make John. F and Jackie O's union look like knees up at the Potters Arms.

Maria was annoyed that George had invited some of the City Infirmary's riff raff to their wedding. Now, she could completely understand why Sister Body and young Sister Dickson were there. They were the respectable backbone of the nursing fraternity. It was a rare treat on their mere nurse's salary to experience such luxury. They didn't know that smoked salmon existed, let alone ever tasted it. She could even understand why her ambitious husband had also invited some of the consultants and their wives, too. Nobody knew better than Maria that to rise through the ranks, it was best to smooth the path on the way. It was always a case of who you knew and not necessarily what you knew within the old boys' network at the hospital. But for the love of God, she could not understand why her groom had insisted on inviting that common barmaid Bren and her even less charming porter of a husband, Tony. They were the spit of leery Sid James and Joan Simms in those vulgar *Carry-On* films that she hated so much. Bren was mutton dressed as lamb that no amount of mascara and jewellery could hide. And there she stood, beaming from the side of the dance floor in her lilac catalogue dress, crumpled fascinator and overpowering perfume. Every time Marie glided past, she got a whiff of her and felt sick. She had chosen to turn a blind eye to her husband's after-work drinking antics within the Potter's Arms, even when George returned stinking of stale beer and the same cheap perfume. In the words of Tammy Wynette, her George was *'just a man'*. Anyway, a lot of the hospital staff called into that public house after a busy day at work for some liquid relief or otherwise. And who could blame them?

Their stiff upper lipped marriage was perfect. They lived the good life without the annoying Tom and Barbara lowering the tone next door. The birth of their first boy, Christian, was the cement that their marriage desperately needed. Since the wedding, George had hardly touched Maria. They both blamed this on their long work hours and responsible jobs. But deep down, they both knew that all was not right in perfect suburbia. In a desperate attempt to rekindle the past, they took an evening stroll down memory lane. It was years since they had smelt the heady scent of fuchsia wafting in the summer evening air as they found their way to the bandstand. But George forgot to sing his

Maria this time around. Nevertheless, baby number two arrived nine months later. Jack was as chunky as his brother. George and Maria loved them both so much. It was just a pity that they didn't love each other with the same passion anymore. With a smile slapped on her face and a nanny firmly on the books, Maria went about her daily business of running a bank, being a mother and appearing as a doting wife.

PC Simcock passed the beautifully manicured lawn and clipped box hedging to arrive at the entrance of this imposing Victorian pile. The gravel under his foot crunched the warning of his arrival at the stained glass door. He didn't want to pull the doorbell or insult the brass knocker with his hand. For a minute or two, he stood, scratching his stubble on the entrance porch, and contemplated his options. He watched two little boys through the panes of leaded glass. Both mites were both only knee height to a grasshopper. They were having a wail of a time pushing each other on a toy bike up and down the Minton-tiled hallway. He didn't want to end the fun of anyone who lived behind this blue door. But sadly, he had no other choice. Sighing deeply, he reluctantly knocked at the door. It was just part of the job and had to be done, no matter how close to home it felt.

As Maria entered the dungeon, the shell of her husband quivered in the corner. She paddled through the urine and lifted his face to meet her eyes. He squinted in the harshness of the fluorescent light as his depravity dawned on her. A firm hand landed on her shoulder from behind. Even in the darkness of this sin, PC Simcock did his best to offer some sort of kindness. Her husband was sick in the head. How could he have done it to her and their two boys? And he was just stupid enough to get caught. That handsome policeman had lured her molly of a husband and arrested him for gross indecency at the urinals. But no, this couldn't be just any public toilet, could it?

Maria felt her pragmatic mind lunge into overdrive. She decided that the first thing to do was to get her gardener to rip any fuchsia bushes out of the borders. She never wanted to see that flower again as long as she lived. The second thing on her list was to shatter that twelve-inch vinyl of *West Side Story*. Thirdly, Maria would damage control. To the outside world, the couple would appear together whilst living their separate lives. Her boys would be none the wiser.

Jack lay in the sand, drilling holes in the warmth below him. He couldn't move without giving the game away. Christian lay beside him in the hot Majorcan sun as they eyed up the local topless talent together. Wham's *I'm Your Man*, drifted out from a radio, punctuating the heavy air of teenage expectation. Christian was nothing more than a horny runt. He was obsessed with lapping up every woman's breasts that bobbed past his eyes and had landed within the Spanish equivalent of 'tit heaven'. He told his younger brother that his next mission was to get his hands on one or two of them. Jack was happy to play along with him. To be honest, he didn't understand what all the fuss was about. Watching the reinforced straps on his mother's bra bellowing on the washing line confirmed this many years ago.

But Jack was playing a dangerous game all of his own whilst his brother was distracted with all things that were nipple related. From the safety of his beach towel, he pretended to be indulging in the same sport as his brother. In the foreground, a bunch of bronzed men were playing a vigorous game of volleyball in the sun. Jack first noticed the unmistakable guttural grunts of masculinity as they served their volleys to each other. And then ping! He couldn't move. It was like being back in the rugby showers again. As he eyed the game in front of him, he was drawn to one blonde long-haired Adonis. He wanted to go over and lick the fresh river of sweat that tantalisingly dribbled towards his waistline. He could almost taste the salty roughness of the man on his cushioned tongue. A few blonde pubic hairs escaped from the man's groin as he lost his balance in the sand. Jack bit his bottom lip. He fought his temptation to slither in between those firm thighs, wipe the sand-tangled blonde hair from his eyes and kiss him.

It wouldn't have been the first time. It was amazing what went on in those showers after a game of rugby. Frothed up in Lynx body wash, Jack's first experience was against the coldness of ceramic tiles. Josh modelled himself on Jason Donavon's Scott in *Neighbours*. He wore a beat-up black biker jacket, bleached jeans and a white t-shirt over his blonde firm frame. But now he was standing proud, stark butt naked and wearing nothing more than a smile. As he got closer, Jack felt the taste of hot breath on his lips. Their playful games of towel flicking had finally changed into something else. Josh's hands made him feel like a Fisher Price activity centre. And from that day, Jack had been conditioned like one of Pavlov's dogs. The mere hint of Lynx shower gel, 'Africa or otherwise, would set him off. Wandering through the aisles of the local chemist store was a big 'no-no'.

As he began to relax, he sat up and noticed his mother. She was sitting alone on the end of a warn wooden jetty, looking out to sea. Even from this distance, he could see that her white embroidered sarong did little to hide the layers of cellulite that hung from her. One hand grappled with a large straw sun hat in the sea breeze. Jack watched her bingo wings wobble and decided to tiptoe through the hot sand to help. It was hard to believe that his mother was once a thing of beauty. His parent's wedding photos looked more like an advertisement for a Hollywood movie. What an earth had happened to her over the years? Now she couldn't advertise SAGA holidays if she even wanted to.

They sat quietly together and stared out to sea. The gentle lap of the froth lulled them into a trance. It wasn't long before they had polished off a jug of sangria. Mum could always be relied upon for liquid refreshments. She was always within arm's length of a glass of wine and some nibbles. They sat breaking bread, dangling their feet in the water whilst shoals of tiny white fish fought for their baguettes. Jack knew his mother was not happy. It had been years since he had seen her properly laugh. Dad was always away on some trip or conference. This Majorcan break was nothing more than a business trip for him. Whilst he spent his time lording it up in the razmataz of the capital city Palma, the rest of them were yet again left to fend for themselves. It was only a month since he had spent a whole week away in San Francisco with Colin, his eager research assistant and full-time prodigy. But this was just not another of his father's business trips. It was the last family holiday together before Jack was leaving for a life in the Royal Air Force. He could even learn to butch it up if it meant that he would get his wings one day.

Turning up at RAF Halton to start the nine weeks of military basic training would be a walk in the park in comparison to the silent war zone of living with his parents. He waved goodbye to his family, paid the obligatory four pounds for the required RAF haircut, and started throwing himself into the training. He tried to stifle a tear of relief as he took his Attestation; an oath of allegiance to the UK monarch that promises duty, diligence, faithfulness and obedience. In time-honoured tradition, there would be nothing subtle about living up to the RAF's motto of 'through adversity to the stars'. His expectations and structured assessments were all set in front of him in the cold light of day to help in his transition from civilian to his new life. And he took to it like a duck to water. The members of his flight were all in the same boat together. For the first time in his life, he felt happy within the shared comradery and support at the base.

The assault courses, inspections, strenuous running and marching were not a problem. Jack had spent months toning his basic level of fitness in preparation for the requirements of his military life. Every night, he had run miles carrying a rucksack full of house bricks in rain or shine. He was not completely phased by the theory either since he was a smart boy, leaving sixth form with A levels in human biology, English and physical education. No, Jack's nemesis was around mastering the ceremonial drill. His poor sense of coordination just got in his way before he finally got the hang of it.

No, this wasn't the blue lockers of the communal flight dormitories. As Jack entered consciousness, he winced and then realised that he was lying in unfamiliar territory. His flight had been deployed to the force protection training area for field assessments, including rifle work, camping, bushcraft and high ropes. The last thing he remembered was lying in the mud in full camouflage gear, firing blanks from a rifle. As he returned to the world of the living, he noticed sticky pads connected to his chest. Someone had shaved his chest hair to make them stick. What was going on? He heard a beep-beep noise to his left and turned to dislodge one of the pads. A loud alert blurted out, triggering immediate assistance to the starched sheets. A man in a crisp white tunic top and RAF epaulettes ran to this bedspace. With electrodes back in place, Jack was instructed to lie still. The nurse assessed the rhythm strip before curtly introducing himself.

"Hello, Jack, I am Corporal Smith. I see that you are awake. You were brought into the medical corps for monitoring as you passed out during the field assessment. At this stage, our tests have shown nothing more serious than hypoglycaemia. We know from your records that you are not diabetic. Your heart is strong and there appears to be no abnormality. However, we want to run a series of further blood works. The results of these investigations will determine your future here."

He then stood silently at the side of his patient, malingering over charting clinical observations, watching the penny drop. Jack sat bolt upright, disturbed the heart trace again and blurted out,

"Are you telling me that if I am not fit then I will be sent home?"

Corporal Smith changed his tactic. Out was regimented ritual and in was kindness. His metal chair scraped along the linoleum as he pulled it closer to his patient. Jack explained that the RAF had given him purpose and pride. For some reason, there was a real acknowledgement in the young corporal's eyes. Jack was given the all-clear, and with the bit between his teeth, he returned to his training.

Jack was having the first in a long line of alcohol-infused epiphanies as he sat swaying at the bar. He realised that he didn't need to fly the planes to feel freedom. All along, he had confused 'freedom' with a need for 'belonging'. And now he had both. Whilst trying not to fall off the bar stool, he leaned over and slurred his first revelation into Corporal Smith's sympathetic ear. He had his whole RAF career in front of him. Well, that is, he would, once he had sobered up from the graduation knees up. And then, Jack had his second epiphany, they seemed to be coming like buses; all at once or none at all. He didn't even know the first name of the man whose ear he had been chewing off all evening. How rude. So he introduced himself all over again. Corporal Smith was bemused by Jack's ham-handed but equally gallant gesture. Smirking, he gripped Jack's left knee before saying,

"Just chill Jack, it's absolutely fine. My name is Darius."

The alcohol flowed as easily as the conversation into the night. Darius explained that he joined the RAF as a student nurse. He had gone to a school career fair and stumbled upon the RAF stand. From that first powerful encounter, there was no stopping him. His mind was set on military nursing, and that was it. He kept his hand in with his NHS counterparts one day a week at the local accident and emergency department. However, his heart belonged to the RAF. He had been on so many fully funded courses to prepare him for the variety of his role. Jack hung onto his every word as Darius explained that he had been on tour to the front line. There was no doubt his head was tightly screwed onto his broad shoulders. Jack sat mesmerised and inspired in equal measures as Darius said that he wanted to apply for officer training in the future. And why not? The RAF is for all, regardless of the colour of your skin.

"I love my job, Jack. Anyone can be anything if you work hard. It's hard to imagine that a boy from a council estate in Birmingham could have been given so much opportunity to grow." He suddenly stopped in mid-flow to take a gulp of lager, wipe the froth from his upper lip and burp. His eyes flickered for a second as if to frame his tale. "My Pentecostal pushing parents were just not my scene. During my time at church, I saw a lot of people prophesied over, claimed to have seen visions, laid on the floor, spoke in tongues, shook, laughed, cried and made animal sounds. They all claimed to be healed by a direct connection with the power of Christ. None of this worked for me. As hard as they tried, they just couldn't exorcise the demon from me."

Following their fill of beer, they staggered back in the general direction of the RAF base, taking a detour through the woods. It was such a balmy evening, and they were in no real rush to get back to the formality of camp. Anyway, it was probably best for them to sober up a little beforehand. The scent of pine hung in the warm evening air as they crushed through the soft bracken. An owl hooted to welcome the two men into its nocturnal world. Jack sat cushioned on a bed of fresh ferns, waiting for Darius to return from behind a large tree trunk. The diuretic effect of lager had its way with his bladder.

He heard Darius singing in a feeble attempt to mask the sound of his urine bursting onto the ground, slurring out *Respect* by Erasure. It must have seeped into his unconsciousness, as it was the last song that they had heard on the pub's jukebox before leaving. *And if I should falter, would you open your...* As Darius appeared from behind the tree trunk smiling in relief, Jack finished his sentence. *...would you open your arms out to me?* He fell beside him, brushing against Jack's leg as he landed. They lay back into the undergrowth in a mass of mess. Staring at the moon through the cracks in the canopy, they finished the next lines of the song together. *We can make love not war and live at peace in our hearts.*

Shit, it was the Lynx Effect all over again. Darius turned and sidled up to him. He stared at the sky, not daring to make eye contact with Corporal Smith. It seemed that Darius had noticed his predicament, too. Without saying a word, he ran his finger over the edge of his top lips. And then, button by button, kiss by kiss, slowly worked his way towards his waist. He teased Jack's hard nipples, making his back arch with an electric shot of pleasure. Darius now straddled him. He removed his shirt to reveal the silhouette of a beautiful ebony torso that shone in the moonlight like a work of muscular art. Jack reached up and gently ran his hand over the firm contours of this man's chest. He weaved his fingers through the crest of short hair that dappled his torso and then pulled his weight on top of him. They were consumed by the slap of skin, the friction of flesh, the wrestle of willing tongues and the connection of their colliding groins.

Coming to his senses, Darius stopped. Jack was too nice for a quick grope, no matter how much he yearned for it. And so they decided to date instead. Occasionally they would steal a weekend away in London, dancing the night away amongst the dry ice and flashing disco lights at Heaven. Sometimes it would be a trip up north to the heady heights of the Flamingo nightclub in Blackpool. No matter where they went, they always kept a watchful eye over their shoulder. They saw young courting couples, who, without thinking, would casually find themselves holding hands. They witnessed older couples in a sequined embrace, spinning each other around the tower ballroom at the tea dances. But their love had to be confined behind closed doors. Being openly gay in Mrs Thatcher's Britain, let alone the RAF, was just not an option.

Jack did some navel gazing and contemplated his career options within the RAF. Following advice and support, he decided to apply for the chance of joining the mobile catering squadron. The mobile catering squadron, or 3MCS, is always the first to arrive on the scene and work. They are experts at providing culinary excellence in one of the world's toughest kitchens. Jack was posted to Worthy Down to start his intense culinary training. He relished in the force protection training as he knew that he had to be ready for anything that feeding the RAF on the frontline could incur. He was honoured and delighted to be part of one of the most intense culinary training courses in the world.

The acrid breath of the military police officer's repulsion filled the stuffy room without even trying. The veins in this man's temples appeared to be on the brink of popping as he tried to keep his composure. Sitting to his left was a military chaplain. He appeared to be far more interested in gazing through the open window, watching the drill sergeants whip their recruits into shape. To his right was the officer in charge of the investigation. The officer pensively tapped his pen on the desk in front of him. Without looking up, he summoned Jack to sit.

All four men were being baked in this tin can together. The whirr of an electric fan offered little relief. Clearing his throat, the officer looked up from his desk and stared Jack directly in the eyes. He then asked,

"Do you have homosexual tendencies?"

He just couldn't lie for one second longer. The deceit was strangling him. Jack was escorted off the camp with no job and no prospects. Darius had vanished off the face of the earth too. Disgraced and rejected, he got on a train and returned to his family home. But the military police had phoned ahead. His father stood in the doorway as Jack crushed up the gravel path. And then George quietly spat,

"You dirty little faggot! Why did you have to go and spoil it for yourself? No, you couldn't keep your stupid mouth shut for just once, could you? There is no place here for someone like you. No sodomite is stepping over my threshold. You are a disgrace. You are dead to both me and your mother."

At this point, Jack's mother appeared from behind her husband. She didn't say a word. The look of disgust on her sallow face said it all. She produced a wad of cash and shoved it in Jack's pocket. As a bank manager, she had always been good with money.

Chapter Sixteen

How do you arrange a funeral if you don't want to say goodbye? After much heartache, we decided on the village church, the missing point in the triangle between the Potters Arms and the hospital. The council had erected a bus shelter on the narrow pavement just outside a steep flight of steps that led up to the churchyard. The funeral corsage followed a Rubik's cube of funeral directors as they tried to solve this puzzle without flagging down the number thirty-two bus with Jack's coffin. Swathed in white roses and lilies, his coffin finally rocked through the cobbled churchyard and into the chapel.

Luckily, the rain had dried up. But pollen mixed with incense set my eyes off again. It was too late for an antihistamine now. Staff were lined up shoulder to shoulder to welcome my man into his resting place. It was lovely that so many of the senior doctors and nurses had turned out to pay their respects. I noticed Sister Dickson and her Consultant Dr Stokes, sitting quietly at the back of the congregation. Sister Body and Dr Taylor were huddled up against them.

Eyes down for a full house. George could predict what the vicar or priest was going to say next as he played funeral bingo. Would it be *The Lord's My Shepard* or *The Old Rugged Cross* this time? And if he heard *Amazing Grace* once more, he would scream. Well, on the inside, anyway. It wasn't that he didn't care; he was just desensitised after all of these years of dabbling in death. But Jane never grew weary of this kind of stuff. It must be something to do with the territory of being a nurse.

Just before the organist started up, Jane rummaged into her handbag and passed over his dry eye drops. It was unusual for George to let down his guard, especially in front of the junior ranks. But nothing was getting past her. Following a discreet application, he smiled warmly and whispered,

"Thank you, Jane, you're an angel. What would I do without you?"

And just before the first few bars of *Abide with Me* lunged into the congregation, Jane smiled, patted his hand and replied,

"Anything for you, George, nobody suspects a thing. But please think about telling Maria. I would hate for her to find out that we are here from somebody else. I'm sick of all these secrets."

He stared blankly at the mahogany coffin, wishing that things could have been different. Anyway, it was too late now for any of that nonsense.

"Merry Christmas, Mrs Douglas," shrieked the rent man.

He watched George through the window, sitting in a tin bath of bubbles, marvelling at a green and silver artificial Christmas tree.

"And let me be the first to wish you a very Merry Christmas too," Mrs Douglas replied.

The heat from frying belly pork and chips dribbled down her neck as she opened the door fully to the confused-looking debt collector. A couple of rogue blue bottles followed her out of the kitchen whilst the rest of them were still taking their chances with the chip pan. Well, what was a bit of extra protein between family? Ginny Douglas was a master of one-pan cooking. On Monday she served chips and egg, Tuesday was chips and sausage, Wednesday was chips and spam, Thursday was chips and chips and then on Friday for a change, she served chips and belly pork. Once the tribe was fed for the week, she topped up the pan with fresh lard and whatever had landed in it. And then the cycle began again. A dollop of fresh dripping slathered over fire-toasted crumpets provided some relief to the lard. Even the odd bit of soot didn't put her off such weekend decadence.

At precisely twelve-thirty every lunchtime, her two grandsons appeared from the cotton mill. These performing sea lions sat at the edge of her crocheted table cloth waiting for the food to be thrown into their mouth. But the cost of their fish, not to mention the rent, had to be paid for somehow. Since her Lenny had died of emphysema, money had been tight. That bloody coal dust got everywhere and in the end, even in his lungs. Smoking thirty roll-ups a day didn't help his cause, but he just wouldn't be told. Either way, Ginny was now left with no money, two hungry grandsons to feed and the rest of a Co-Op funeral to pay for. Even the divvy didn't stretch that far.

The answer to her prayers was greased by a beautiful young couple who had just moved into the maisonette above her. Surely they would need a little help with something. How on earth did Mrs Taylor spend all day on her feet, washing, curling and backcombing the local hoity-toity when nearly eight months pregnant? On many occasions, Ginny saw her standing behind the salon window with one hand on her back and the other on a curling iron. It was a wonder how she still managed to have Mr Taylor's tea on the table every night when he finished working as an accountant at the City Infirmary. But when George popped his head into the world, Ginny Poppins was born to step in and plug the gap. George was just more than a way of feeding her family. She sat for hours cuddling him from her crimplene frock, loose curlers and hairnet. When the troops had their fill, it was time to lull her little 'Georgie Pudding and Pie' to his afternoon nap. Only when he was sound asleep and gurgling on her breast would she get up from the rocking chair?

George was as happy as a pig in muck when 'Ma Ma Douglas' was looking after him. He could be anything he wanted to be with her, within reason. He loved nothing more than rummaging through her Aladdin's Cave of clothes. Her three-door wardrobe was so large that he was able to go in one door and come out of another. Sometimes, he fell asleep in the musty mothballs and shoe boxes that lined the bottom of this treasure trove. Ginny never batted an eyelid if he appeared wearing one of her fake furs, her Sunday best dress or slingbacks as long as the make-up was removed before he went home. And more to the point, if he wanted to go for a hearthside paddle in the middle of August to the backdrop of a Christmas Tree, then who was she to deny him?

But there was one thing that scared George more than anything. Growing up in the shadow of a rat-infested railway bank played havoc with his nerves. Every time the coal waggons trundled past, their nests were disturbed. Many a time he heard their piercing shriek as father pounded them to death with two blooded house bricks that he kept especially for the occasion. Controlling the vermin on the outside of the flat was one thing, but finding a nest of naked babies in the back of the scullery was a whole different level of torture. From that day onwards, he slept with one eye open. It was this fear that spurred George on to make something of himself. He didn't want to waste his life behind a desk like his father or develop varicose veins like his poor mother. Those leg ulcers killed her, but still she stood in compression bandages, trying to act as if she gave a damn about her customers.

Joining the boy scouts was a stroke of luck. Not only did he get to learn new skills, but got the chance to go away to camp. George sat by the campfire, whittling his stick into a spear. A smoky voice cracked over the embers and startled him. Damn it, he had nicked his finger now. As George sucked his cut, a lad said,

"Sorry George, I didn't mean to frighten you. Did you cut yourself? Are you Ok?"

"Don't worry, I'll live Dylan. It's not your fault. I was miles away."

Now looking at George's creation, he asked, "What an earth are you carving, anyway? I don't think there are many vampires around here."

"I'm whittling this stake to keep anyone away who wakes me up, pulls off my blanket and flaps around on top of me like a demented ghost. Does that ring any bells?"

"George, I have no idea what you are on about. Are you making these stories up again in your head?"

The two lads burst into a belly-laughing fit before retiring for another night under canvas. Only the tent separated them from the summer squelch. Bats' wings banged in the air as insects drilled into the earth. George sat bolt upright and grabbed hold of his stake. There was no way he could sleep now, as the sound of something filthy had just scurried past his head.

"Dylan, are you awake? I can't sleep. I think it was a rat or something even worse?"

"Well, I am now George. When are you going to learn that they won't hurt you? I have been trying to tell you that for the last ten years, but you won't have it."

"I'm too hot to sleep anyway now. Do you fancy a swim?"

With the stealth of a couple of bank robbers, the lads crept past the scoutmaster's tent before they were stopped. George placed his arm around Dylan's shoulder whilst his eyes adjusted to the darkness. There was no way he would be a midnight snack for a passing vampire or werewolf. After all, it was a full moon. Before they knew it, they had arrived at the lake. Some kind soul had conveniently built a wooden jetty out into the water for them. Tied canoes banged against the current, demanding to be let loose. But the boys had other ideas. They ran towards the moon, stark butt naked and arm in arm. George felt the coolness of the breeze, the rough planks beneath his feet and the smoothness of Dylan's biceps linking his. For a second they were weightless before hitting the inky water. At this precise moment, there was no one telling him what to do, how to act, or what to say. There was no Maria to play along with, no parents to please, and definitely no Sunday school. All that remained was the shrivelled truth, freedom and Dylan.

"Let's go for a float. It normally calms you down," Dylan suggested.

"Ok then, but you won't let go of me will you. I don't want to be taken by the current?"

Before he knew what had happened, George had been swept up and was now holding his friend's hand as they drifted through the water, watching the moon together.

The din of a spoon banging on a saucepan span George back into the land of the living. He had slept so well on their return to camp. A frenzy of activity rocked the tents as the troop of lads tried to dress and report for breakfast. Well, calling it breakfast was a stretch to be honest, unless burnt porridge served into square tins qualifies. Following their fill of rust, it was time for another hike in blister-hugging boots. The scout leader explained that the lads would be in for a spot of bivouac-making, once they had trudged through the wilderness using only their compasses for direction. But was this all necessary? As a rule, George never went any more bush than a grope with Maria. The Queen's Park wasn't exactly the Outer Hebrides by any stretch of the imagination. And then he flinched, thought about the alternatives and just got on with it. Anything was better than those railway rats.

Before he knew it, George was face down, tasting mud. He wouldn't cry, even though every bone in his body hurt. Dylan reached down to help him up. An angry voice shouted,

"Don't help him up Dylan, leave that arse bandit where he belongs."

"Ok Tom, hang on a minute and let me catch up with you."

And now more than George's bones hurt as he watched his friend sprint to catch up with the thugs who were leading their orienteering exhibition. Eventually, he got out of the mud, dusted himself off, and followed the rest of the boys. Looking worried, Dylan turned back and silently mouthed,

"Are you all right, George?"

But it was too late. George had enough of being played with.

"Well, what time do you call this then, lads? I've been waiting for hours. Now that you have finally made an appearance, it's time for the second activity," beamed the ruddy ginger-haired scoutmaster.

He paired the lads together without giving it much thought. Well, they were sharing the same tent and seemed close. George harvested a bracken camouflage whilst Dylan crudely erected a triangle-shaped frame made from fallen branches. Cocooned like two squirrels, the boys lay silently, listening to the rain drip through their creation with only a blanket to keep them warm. Dylan cleared his throat, moved a strand of undergrowth from his face and whispered,

"George, I'm so sorry, I'm just not like you."

"In what way are we different? I didn't hear you protest last night when you rubbed on top of me. You never complain when my hand is down your pants either."

"I'm not a puff like you George, I like girls too.,"

"Well, who do think Maria is then? She isn't a figment of my imagination." George barked back.

I'm just sorry, George, my head is all over the place."

George felt the soil tremble beneath them. As he glanced over, he saw Dylan was silently sobbing. So he did what he always did when Dylan was playing up. He simply pulled him closer until he was tucked in his chest for the night. He rested his head on top of his, hugged him tightly and breathed in the mixture of desperation, mud and sweat. Before they knew what they were doing, both lads had somehow managed to nod off.

Everything looked better in the morning warmth. Glints of fresh sun fragmented through the canopy as the morning flap of birds chirped that it was the end of this ordeal. George tasted dry spit on his tongue, released his lover from his grip and stretched. Dylan had been dragged through a hedge backwards with bits of God only knows what stuck to him. George couldn't kiss properly, but all the same offered a cracked lip. Nothing is more innocent than a new day unfolding in the forest. The morning sun broke through the trees, offering shards of expectation. George smelt freshly watered pine in the air. The hum of waking insects grew louder as the forest's natural thermostat was turned up. All of this had gone on for thousands of years without mother nature giving it a second thought. Still a little clumsy, they clanked their belongings together and stomped towards the smell of a fire burning in the clearing.

Sitting on a log, scraping congealed oats from a tin canny, Tom piped up,

"Well, if it isn't the two lovebirds. I see that you have kissed and made up."

"Change your record, idiot," Dylan spat.

"Make me, you filthy shirt lifter."

In a split second, they were face-down, wrestling in the mud. A rip of shirts, a rub of muscles, a grunt of pain, and finally submission. Dylan had pinned Tom to the ground and now they faced each other. But Tom didn't attempt to move from his captor's grip.

Dylan parted his thick brown mop, brushed his teeth and smelled his breath on his hand. It was hard to see where his milky complexion began, and his porcelain muscles ended. If it wasn't for the crisp blue shirt and navy tie, he would have been lost in the mirror. He felt two gentle hands on his hips guiding him away from the vanity unit. George quickly ran his hands through his fine blonde hair. Luckily, it fell into a pageboy cut without much trouble. They were cutting it fine. The ward round would be starting sharp in ten minutes. Grabbing their white coats and stethoscopes, the men raced to the medical ward. Dr Wagner did not suffer fools, staff who asked too many questions or late medical students. Everything and everyone had a place at the City Infirmary and woe betide them if they crossed the line. With seconds to spare, Dylan and George landed on the ward. Jane crept up behind them and straighten their collars before Dr Wagner had time to notice. She giggled, winked and then trotted back into the sluice to carry on with cleaning the stainless steel bedpans. By the time she was finished, her patients would be able to see their faces, let alone anything else, in them. Jane didn't mind what she was asked to do. It was all part of her life as a student nurse. As long as she was helping, it didn't matter if she was folding starched sheets, cutting up bandages or on the back round. This two hourly ritual involved turning immobile patients to prevent pressure sores, washing their back (including anything else that needed attention) and changing the bed if needed. Armed with a bowl of hot water, a bar of soap and a trolly, two nurses would go from bed to bed until the task was complete, changing the soap at the end of the round. Although this task was much like painting the Fourth Bridge, she was able to grab a quick word with each patient before moving on.

Dr Wagner stared down his pointed nose and blurted out,

"You see, Das is right, patient has pneumonia."

Thank goodness for that. At least George hadn't been publicly humiliated again in the middle of the ward. The nurses still playfully called him 'Dat imbecile' three weeks later, and now, it was Dylan's turn to face his fate. He gently introduced himself to Larry and gained his consent before proceeding. If only he had a pound for every time a patient said, 'Yes as long as you warm your stethoscope first'. Larry had been admitted to the medical ward with coal miner's lung. His chronic obstructive bronchitis was playing havoc with his bagpipes, which now wheezed a song of their own every time he tried to speak. The nurses had been administering hot steam via the Dr Nelson's earthenware inhalation every few hours, but his sputum just wasn't shifting and had now turned a nasty shade of green. Dylan took Larry's history through his broken sentences. Then he carried on to inspect, palpate, percuss and auscultate this poor man's barrel chest, under the scrutiny of Dr Wagner. Turning to the Consultant, Dylan delivered a diagnosis of infective bronchitis. And much to the Senior physician's annoyance, this arrogant medical student was spot on. Dr Wagner sprayed the ward round as he announced,

"Gut, you are correct," and then he stopped, smirked and continued, "So no imbecile today, ya? Well done boyz. We may make doctors ov you both yet."

But Dr Wagner was right, both George and Dylan flew through medical school training together.

Maria and George, Dylan and Jane made such a cosy foursome. Jane scrimped and saved to buy the ball dress of her dreams. Her sapphire floral embroidered tulle sheer mesh neck rockabilly swing-A-line number was perfectly complemented by a pair of suede kitten heals, a lacquered brown bouffant with a matching headband and a string of pearls. Jane had gone to town in a crimson full-length, V-neck spaghetti strap satin number, a black backcombed beehive and a jaw-dropping ruby rhinestone drop leaf necklace with matching earrings. The boys had scrubbed up so well too. Maria went weak in the knees when she saw her George turn the corner in full black tie. His golden hair shimmered to the glow of the glitter ball as they sashayed onto the dance floor. Jane awkwardly grabbed hold of Dylan's black tuxedo and followed their friends to the perfectly sprung floor. All of those months of practising ballroom dancing on the bandstand in the Queen's Park had finally paid off. Not a single toe was stepped on as they glided along to Engelbert Humperdinck's *The Last Waltz*. Admiring senior nurses and medical staff sat in carousel formation to the side of the dance floor as this year's gaggle of junior doctors took their rightful place in the Infirmary's Hall of Fame. Even Dr Wagner managed to crack a smile from his withered face and dusty grey hair before turning to speak to his rather robust wife. George didn't know if he was being swept up in the traditional venue or by a couple of pints of Dutch courage that were swirling around inside him. Either way, he leaned into Maria's lacquer, narrowly missing getting caught up in her earing and whispered,

"The most beautiful sound I ever heard, Maria. I have never seen you look more beautiful than you do tonight. One of these days, I am going to marry you and we will have the biggest wedding that the

Infirmary has ever seen. I will whisk you around this dance floor with all eyes on you, my darling."

"Oh George, do you mean that?"

"All the beautiful sounds in a single word. Maria, Maria, Maria," he sang in her ear lobe before she melted in his arms.

Although they looked the part, the University Grand Hall was not having the same effects on Dylan and Jane. For months they had tried dating, but any attempts of heavy petting only led to fits of laughter. Maybe they just knew each other too well for romance to spark. Jane was like a fish out of water in her evening dress; that bloody boned corset cut her in two every time she tried to move. What sadist had invented such a contraption? Following some light refreshments and speeches from a musty old medical professor and an even mustier matron, the formality of the evening degenerated into a party. Whilst there was nothing wrong with a bit of Cilla Black, the Beatles or indeed The Beach Boys, George and Dylan left the girls on the dance floor and headed to the bar. After another round or two, they swayed in the general direction of the gent's toilets.

The lads tried to remain upright whilst standing at the urinal with one hand on the wall and the other on their dicks watching piss trickle into the drain. George coughed and vomited down the porcelain, whereas Dylan just managed to turn around and collapse in a cubicle before spewing his ring up. Once relieved of smoked salmon and dill vol-au-vent and six pints of beer, George grabbed Dylan, pulled him to his feet, locked the cubicle, turned him around, unzipped his trousers, and gave him his graduation present. Now done with each other, Dylan turned around, looked his lover coolly in the eyes, and said,

"That's my goodbye gift, George. I love you with all my heart, but I won't be second fiddle to Maria anymore."

"No, please, I love you too. What do you mean?" George cried whilst pulling up his trousers.

"You told her that you wanted to marry her. I almost choked on her words when she told me. But don't worry, I didn't blow your cover, unlike your cock. You've made your choice. I'm leaving in the morning".

Dylan left his lover crying in the cubicle with the taste of him still on his body. And just like that, he was gone the next morning without so much as a letter or an explanation.

George didn't know if getting caught or facing Maria was worse. The Policeman was so convincing as he smiled seductively through the corner of his moist mouth, flicked back his brown mop of hair and stared longingly at his dick. Even the stench of overflowing piss from the broken drain didn't put him off. He brushed his hand past George's thigh and led him to the safety of the cubicle. The stranger was as hard as he was deceitful. But instead of copping a mouthful of throbbing cock, George felt his cuffs instead. No matter what he said or what he did, Maria would never forgive him. And he didn't blame her one bit for calling him sick, abnormal, degenerate and worse, for after all, he was. All of these years he had lied to her and rubbed it in her face. But for the sake of the children, she would have him back. The boys would never know or be any of the wiser. Well, it was for better, for worse, wasn't it?

She didn't complain when he had given her the biggest wedding that the Royal Infirmary had ever seen. And he even managed to go through with the wedding reception to please her. Every time his eyes wandered over to the door to the left of the bar, he thought of his graduation. But still, he smiled, like the perfect groom as he whisked her around the dancefloor. The only realness at this pantomime was

Tony and Bren. At least he could just be himself with this couple. They didn't judge or expect anything from him.

George sat on a green-painted bench under the shade of a tree overlooking the nursing home, trying to make sense of the last ten hours of working as a junior doctor in the cancer ward. Taking a drag from a roll-up, he contemplated a career in oncology. Was he strong enough to delve into death daily? Could he make a difference and was he cut out for all of this? Deep into his thoughts, he never noticed a ginger-haired porter trundle past with the empty trolley until it was too late.

"Don't worry, it is empty this time. I have just come back from the mortuary and am on my way to pick up another customer from your ward, Dr Taylor. Oh, sorry to disturb you, are you Ok?"

"Yes, thank you, Tony. I was just getting my head together. It's tough in there sometimes."

"Then why don't you call into the 'Potters Arms' on your way home, then? My wife Bren works behind the bar. I'm sure that after a couple of pints, you will feel better."

George could smell warm beer and friendship as he opened the door to the boozer. Under a fairy-lit glow, Tony stood in a leather jacket, white rippled T-shirt and spray-on bell-bottom jeans, waving him over to the bar. He felt his firm hand on the arch of his back as they said hello. And as if by magic, his wife Bren appeared, leaned over the bar to show her low-cut cleavage, and laughed. As she threw her arms at him he could smell her heavy perfume, hear her jewellery jangle and feel her long purple talons touch his shoulders. She pulled him a pint whilst the three of them got acquainted. Over the din of the pub and the plumes of smoke, Tony explained,

"Bren, this is the one and only Dr George Taylor I was telling you about earlier. I found him moping around outside the oncology ward earlier today, looking far too serious for my liking. I knew you would cheer him up. Look at him. He is far too handsome to be miserable, isn't he?"

And after a few pints, George was feeling a little more relaxed. He could feel Tony's leg vibrate against the side of his bar stool as they put the world to right. He didn't even mind it when a hand landed on the back of his stool, catching hold of his belt to stop him from falling. By now, George was resting his elbows on the bar towels, listening in fascination as the couple explained that they were swingers. George had never heard of anything of the like before but understood instantly. It was as if he was sitting in the confessional box. Everything to do with Dylan and Maria came tumbling out of his head and onto the bar. Instead of penance, Bren served another pint as Tony's hand got a little firmer on his buttocks. Last orders came and went. Bren hugged her patrons and wished them good night, locked the pub door, turned off the lights and welcomed Dr George Taylor to their world. George was like a dog with two dicks and spoilt for choice. But for the first time in his life, he didn't have to choose.

As he stared at his son's coffin, George thought about the last time he had seen him alive and what he had said. And then he cried again. This was just something that he would carry to his own grave.

Even Carla and Vivien sobbed in the back row of the oak pews as we walked down the central aisle of the chapel. *Abide With Me* battered out from a dusty organ to welcome us. Wayne grabbed hold of my arm as we staggered to the front of the chapel. Father Gregson, our local vicar, welcomed us into his home. Since he also moonlighted at the hospital and knew Jack, it felt right that he should conduct the service. He gently rested his hand on the mahogany coffin and began to speak. With a twinkle in his eye, he described Jack's humour, his fierce protection, his selflessness, but most of all, the love that he shared for us all. Next came a sodden speech from Adam,

"I wasn't with Jack for all that long, we were robbed of that chance, but I truly loved him and he loved me in return. He loved me without judgement. He saw the real me, which is hypocritical coming from a drag queen, I know. I didn't need to be anyone else other than myself around him. The drag is an illusion, our love, although fleeting, was real. I wanted to get old with him, sit on the porch, hold his hand and watch the sun go down in the distance. I wanted to build a lifetime of photo albums with him. But he was just too good for this world. I'm sorry, I..."

And then he sat before he fell. It was my turn to stand up and say a few words. Snuffling through a cracked voice, I said,

"You will have to excuse me all. These blinking flowers are playing havoc with my sinuses. But I guess Jack would find that funny. I don't know what to say or what to tell you to be completely truthful. From the moment we met, we just clicked. He was the brother I never had, the older sister I yearned for, and the joker who could make me laugh. There are many stories that I could share with you, but they probably aren't appropriate in God's house, so just know one thing: I love you, Jack."

Danni grabbed hold of my hand as I sat back in between her and Wayne. She whispered to me,

"Thank you, Max, I don't know how you did that. It was beautiful."

Dolly Parton's *I Will Always Love You* drifted across the mourners. Father Gregson gave a beautiful and meaningful sermon. He told us that in God's house we were all welcome. Perhaps heaven was similar to the European Drag Bar then. Maybe Saint Peter leaned provocatively over those pearly gates, in a blonde wig, an iridescent bodice and three-inch heels to welcome Jack. I could hear him as Mae West saying, "Awe, awe, come up and see me sometime." It was not as if anyone could prove the fact either way. Instead of celestial harps, perhaps Jack is playing his backing tambourine on a cloud right now. Grief is odd, it makes you think about the weirdest things. It was probably best if I kept these thoughts to myself, for now at least anyway.

We followed Jack's coffin as it bounced out of the chapel and to the local crematorium. I have no idea how we got to this soulless place. If it wasn't for the one in, one out precession of coffins, this building could have been mistaken for a council office block. I just hoped that an elderly lady hadn't tried to pay her rent here in error, getting more than she had bargained for. I wanted to be sick. Who had told Paul and Daniel that Jack was dead? But this wasn't the time and place for my drama for once. Coolly, I nodded at them without uttering a word, grabbing tighter onto Wayne and Danni. Cremations are weird. Everyone, with the exemption of the star turn, knows why they are there and what is going to happen, but still, it is gut-wrenching when the podium is lowered and the curtains are drawn at the end of the performance. Not even Bette's *Wind Beneath My Wings* could soften this blow.

Some of the hospital staff followed us back for a customary cheese bap and sausage roll that was served at the Potters Arms. Danni, Wayne and I sat huddled together holding court at our usual table, getting drunker as the staff gave their respects and plied us with booze. It is so difficult to find the right words to say in these situations, I get it, but if

I heard 'I'm so sorry for your loss' and 'What a beautiful sendoff' one more time, I was going to get up on the bar and scream. Aunt Bren and Dr Taylor were getting louder by the minute. Their infectious laughter rang around the bar and filled the boozer. Adam stopped by to chat with the couple on the way to the gents and appeared to be fuelling whatever was going on. But far better this honest emotion than stilted condolence. I had no idea what they were laughing about, but if it worked for them, then it worked for me.

Bren leaned into George and said,

"Are you Ok darling, what is wrong? It's been a long time, hasn't it, but here we are again. I have lost my Tony, and you have lost your son."

"What! How the hell did you know, Bren? Oh my God, who else knows?"

"You should know me better than that by now, George. I may be a lot of things, but I know when to keep my mouth shut. It didn't take me long to put two and two together. Can you see Max over there sitting with Danni and Wayne? Well, he's my nephew and tells me everything. To be honest, he's more like a son to me. Your son was more like a brother to him. They were thick as thieves. Just like you, George, he is so cut up by his death. Did you know that Jack was admitted to his ward when he was on duty? He won't tell me, but I'm sure he blames himself in some way."

George moved in a little closer to Bren, wiped the tears away, and said,

"I am such a fucking idiot. If only I hadn't been such a sanctimonious twat, life could have been so different. I blame myself for knocking every nail in my boy's coffin."

"Well, you weren't thinking straight, were you? Don't beat yourself up, what is done is done. Now Dr Taylor, go to the bar and buy me another drink. I am sure that you can afford it on your consultant wage. And let me make it clear, it is only a drink that I want from you."

They burst into another fit of giggles as George jumped up, saluted her, and swayed over to his old perch at the bar.

Going back to the ward was much easier than I expected. Much to my nursing family's relief, I found comfort in being around the environment where I had seen Jack alive for the last time. It was as if we were still connected. I would often talk to him in my head as I went about my nursing business on the unit. I could hear him mimic Bruce Forsyth saying 'Didn't she do well' at the end of the Generation Games' conveyer belt sequence as he watched me.

But Danni was my voice of reason. All of my best decisions had been taken from The Potters Arms, so why should things change now? Wayne watched a game of ping-pong play out between Danni and me. Sister Jackie was taking a change of direction and was leaving the neuroscience ward. There would be an opening for a new junior sister/charge nurse. These posts were like gold dust and attracted only the crème de la crème of nurses. By the fifth pint, my mind was made up. I would go for it. I was suited and booted and ready to spring into action once again. But there was an administrative error resulting in all three candidates showing up at the same time. We sat together and made small talk as, one by one, we took turns to trail into the floor show. The panel asked all the usual clinical, leadership, and professional questions. There was nothing about the interview that either surprised or threw me. It was just a very matter-of-fact process to score well on each question. Because, as Bruce Forsyth and Jack always said, 'Points make prizes'.

It turned out that all three of us had performed equally well at the interview. The problem was just that; we had all performed *equally* well. The situation was solved by putting us in a room together where

HOW CAN WE BE WRONG?

we were left to decide who would get the job. I was flabbergasted. And in that single moment, I lost all respect for the neuroscience senior leadership team. The other candidates were people whom I had worked alongside for years. We had shared blood, sweat, and tears together. How could you pick a favourite child? What on earth was going on? Anger rose from the pit of my stomach. Puckering out my chest and turning on my heel, I stormed into the panel and told them that it was over. I was not a pawn in their hunger games. And with that, I left Sharron Varley's office with my dignity intact and a month's notice on her desk. What had I done now? In the blink of an eye, Wayne and I had sold up and were moving to London together to start the next chapter in our relationship.

Chapter Seventeen

'Bittersweet memories, that is all I'm taking from me, so goodbye, please don't cry,' rung out over the mourners. But it was too late. Danni was crying. She just couldn't keep it together. *'And I'm wishing you joy and happiness, but most of all, I'm wishing you love'.* She sat frozen to the spot and watched Jack's coffin at the front of the Church. Max slumped down beside her after delivering his beautiful eulogy. For once, she was lost for words, *'And I will always love you, I will always love you'.* How could she make sense of the senseless? As she sat on the hard pew in the candlelight, a thousand memories flooded her brain.

"Bugger, bugger, bugger, bugger," he shouted at the top of his shrill voice as Sally entered the house. She had visited to complete a dementia care assessment. But he was having none of it. His feathers were ruffled and that was that. His beady black eyes darted as Sally and her well-meaning smile sunk into the brown draylon sofa next to him. This was not going to be an easy assessment with all this commotion going on. He now blurted out his other favourite word at her, "Shit, shit, shit, shit," over and over again.

Jane entered the room with a tray of tea and biscuits, half laughing and apologising at the same time. In all of the kerfuffle of caring for her father with dementia, working part-time as a home help, running a household, being a wife to Peter and a mother to nine-year-old Danni, she had completely forgotten that Sally was visiting today. This workhorse was normally good at plate spinning, but her hand now trembled as she poured the tea. It was difficult playing mother with one hand whilst trying to throw a blanket over Percy's cage with the other. Smiling in embarrassment, Jane confessed that her father had ruined that 'bloody parrot'.

Jimmy had always been a comic at heart. He had a knack for making his presence known as he entered any room without saying a single word. And when he did speak through that soft Irish lilt, he was just hilarious. The family tried to persuade him to enter Opportunity Knocks because he would break Hughie Green's clapometer with his banter. Long before dementia had set in, Jimmy had spent many a happy hour teaching Percy how to swear. Like a naughty schoolboy, he spluttered in delight at the visitor's reactions to the parlour trick. He may have ruled the roost in Westfield, but Jimmy was certainly not allowing Father Percival to throw his sanctimonious weight around here. There were different rules in the United Kingdom. Father Percival would learn to knock before entering the house. If he would not, then Percy would trumpet his arrival across the threshold with a fanfare of obscenity. Either way, it was a win-win in Jimmy's eyes.

With Percy securely tucked away, the assessment could finally begin. Jane was unsure about opening up to Sally. Although she worked as a home help herself, it all felt strangely invasive on the receiving end. What did this open-sandaled bit of a wench know about life? But from under her tie-dye kaftan and matching headband, Sally quickly got to the heart of the matter. In a nutshell, Jane was struggling to care for her dad as his dementia was progressing. And who could blame her?

Jimmy worked all of his adult life in the local pottery industry. Jane explained that her dad had emigrated from the west coast of Ireland to make a better life for himself. He met his Mavis amongst the china dust and lust of youth. He was the Saggar maker's bottom knocker to her slip glazer. Jane jubilantly appeared seven months after the happy couple had tied the knot. She caught hold of her words and stopped speaking for a second, worrying that she had said too much already. Losing her mother to cancer a couple of years earlier was bad enough but this was a whole new ball game. At least her mother's death was over and done with quickly.

Sally saw that the family was struggling. Jimmy had wandered from the family home despite their best efforts to keep him safe. He had been picked up by the local bobbies on four occasions already. As soon as the sun went down, he sprang into action. On one recent occasion, he had turned up at the local primary school with an orange in his hand. Luckily, it was parents' evening, so the school was still full as he arrived. In his mind, all he wanted to do was to make sure that his daughter Karen was not hungry. He thought that he had forgotten to give eight-year-old Karen her lunch before she left for school. Luckily, with a bit of detective work, the teachers realised who Jimmy was. Although a couple of generations later, it was a godsend that Karen's daughter was a pupil at the very same primary school.

Sally understood what Karen needed. And more to the point, she had the resources at her fingertips to put her plan into swift action. She wanted to keep Jimmy safe at home for as long as she could. The last thing he needed was a move from the familiarity and comfort of his own family. And then she revealed her three-point plan. Transport would pick Jimmy up for daycare three times a week. The family would also receive an evening care sitter twice a week. This respite would allow Jane, her husband, and Danni to still go out together as a family. And more to boot, all of this wrap-around would be free of charge. Sally also arranged for regular GP and health visitor checkups. It was wonderful. Jane cried in relief that social services and the national health service were working seamlessly to support and help them.

With her best handwriting, Danni wrote her letter to Father Christmas and carefully placed it up the sooty chimney. On Christmas morning Danni found a beautifully wrapped present with her name on it. She gently prised it from under the multi-coloured fairy lights that hung from the silver tinsel artificial Christmas tree, almost bursting with excitement. This gift was everything that she wanted and more. It even came with a plastic stethoscope, a fob watch, a bandage, and a toy syringe. She loved her little pale blue dress and white nurse's cap so much. Danni decided that her outfit was her second favourite thing in the whole world. Grandad Jimmy was always number one as she worshipped the ground that he shuffled upon. They sat for hours playing together on the tufted hearth rug.

But junior nurse Danni was in total control. She had all of her teddy bears and dolls lined up in perfectly perpendicular precision as she strutted up and down the central aisle of her nightingale ward. From this central point, she was able to attend to the needs of her patients. Skilfully examining Big Ted she decided he needed to be treated for a severe case of contagious fur bottom again. That would teach him for playing out in the rain without his coat. It took her a little longer to diagnose her next casualty, though. Miss Barbie Doll was a tricky one to sort out. She defied medical science. Playing with the bobbles in her blonde pigtails, nurse Danni decided that she would need to consult with Dr Grandad Jimmy. After all, he was the resident expert in all things doll related. Together they arrived at the evidence-based diagnosis that poor Barbie had a terminal case of split-ended pink leg. They would have to operate immediately if she was going to live.

Danni knew that her Granddad Jimmy was finding it harder to keep up with the antics of the fireside hospital ward. Now and again, he was lost in an empty gaze. When Grandad looked unravelled, she simply took hold of his hand and gently soothed him. Sometimes it took him a little longer to return to her. When he had been gone for too long, she calmly sang one of his favourite songs. Jane was so proud that her nine-year-old daughter knew all of the words of Vera Lynn's, *I'll Be Seeing You*. Usually, by the last lines of the song, *I'll find you in the morning sun, And when the night is new, I'll be looking at the moon, I'll be seeing you,* Grandad was back in the room. And then the day arrived that he sadly wasn't.

Danni couldn't do right for doing wrong. The nurse tutors were always hearing from the regimented ward staff that she spent more time talking to the patients than getting on with her work. A hospital ward was not a place for idle chit-chat. As only a slip of a student nurse herself, she knew that she was in no position to challenge the status quo. Well, not just yet anyway. She seethed from underneath her pinned blonde hair and blue and white checked student uniform when made to fold sheets instead of comforting the sick. These traditionalists may win the battle, but one day Danni would win the war.

She struck up an unlikely relationship with Paul. He caught her attention straight away during a placement together within the A and E. Amongst the walk-in wounded, the visiting vagrants and the genuine emergencies, she was coyly struck by his swimmer body and long blonde hair. They were always stuck on the same Obs and gobs round together. This unflattering terminology was given to the task of providing oral care to the patients who were unable to do this for themselves, coupled with taking their blood pressure, pulse, and temperature. Danni and her fellow students were trained to break all nursing procedures into rounds of task allocation. It wasn't a patient needing care, it was a series of military necessity. Student nurses always got the jobs that no one wanted to do. But Danni spent many of a happy hour being the bath nurse for the day. People were wheeled into her on a conveyor belt to be washed and scrubbed. But she learnt far more about them in the intimate moments of the Chinese Laundry than within the cavernous ward areas. For Danni, it wasn't just a bath, it was therapy.

Her feeble attempts at flirting with Paul didn't land well. Instead of gaining love, she settled for friendship instead. She had no idea that he was gay. When she thought about it, she had never met an openly gay person before. They must have existed, she was sure of it. It was just something that wasn't talked about in polite conversation with her mother and father over tea. Never did her father say, "Can you pass me the salt please Jane, by the way, a lovely gay couple have moved in two doors down." To be completely honest, her parents had pretty much avoided any serious conversations. It wasn't until she got to nursing school that she learned about the birds and the bees. Paul found it endearing that Danni was not worldly-wise. As their friendship developed, he made it his mission to educate her on how the world worked in all of its glory. They were like two peas within the same pod. They often put the world right over a pint in the Potter's Arms after a busy day on the wards. Danni was a cheap date. It only took a whiff of the barmaid's apron to have her slurring like a drunkard. Over the din of happy drinkers, she announced that,

"One day, you will see, I will become a ward Sister. And when that day arrives, there will be no room for frilly hats and fear."

Once qualified, this lioness was finally let out of her clinical cage. Off were the kid gloves and in was her trademark spiky blonde confidence. Rising at a rate of knots through the nursing hierarchy was not easy while keeping hold of her core values. But like a dose of laxatives, Danni was determined to purge the City Infirmary. Within four years of qualifying, she had risen to the dizzy heights of an intensive care Sister. But her dreams were even bigger. Instead of being a big fish in a little pond, she made the risky decision to swim with the sharks to change future generations of nursing practice. When the Director of Nursing gave her a break, she nearly bit his hand off before he got the chance to sever hers clean. But Danni would always be a nurse shark and never a great white. She was responsible for training healthcare assistants. Under her instruction, this new lilac-clad army would be taught to always put the patient at the centre of what they did.

Wearing her parrots, she strutted into the health care support training school ready to whip her troops into action. They were such a diverse group of people. But one student was clearly out of his depth and stared like a startled rabbit out from the safety of his plastic chair. Awe, bless him, naivety on a stick. Jack would look after him, come to think of it. Where was he, anyway? That boy would be late for his own funeral, given half the chance. Both Paul and Danni had warned him that there would be dire consequences if he wasn't on time. Right, that was it. She was left with no choice but to call his bluff; a deal is a deal. It would be such a shame if his nickname slipped from her mouth over lunch.

The first two weeks of health care training school went like a dream. There was only one day in the programme that could have gone one way or the other. She almost wet herself when that tart jubilantly sprang from behind the curtain, wearing nothing more than his tight blue budgie smugglers and a smile. He was going to live up to his reputation as Miss Australia if it killed him. As Jack jumped on the bed in front of the group, she waited for his next move and fought back her laughter as he announced in a poor American slur,

"Tonight Danni, I'm going to be Tammy Wynette and I'll be singing *Stand By Your Bed*."

Luckily he refrained from turning her class into a drag show. Well, Jack had warned her that he would get his own back on her one way or another.

In between teaching health care support workers, Danni kept her hand in by helping out on any of the wards that would have her. This was a great way to find out what went on behind the looking glass. But she got more than she bargained for during a shift in A and E one night. When the cardiac arrest was over, the staff went out for a fag, regardless of whether they smoked or not. There was a discreet hidey hole behind a corrugated cargo tank. From the road, it looked like staff had been called to conclave to elect a pope. No amount of nicotine could soothe Dr Stokes' nerves that evening. He just couldn't get the image of that dead eight-year-old boy out of his mind. He saw his blood-stained body with the endotracheal tube still thrust into his throat. Despite the resuscitation team's desperate efforts, the boy was already too beaten and abused to survive CPR. As John leaned back against the wall sobbing, someone sidled up against him. Without thinking, he turned, leaned in, and placed a kiss on her lips.

Danni was infatuated with him. John was as tender on the inside as he was firm on the outside. In all honesty, they just couldn't keep their hands off each other. Suddenly Danni wasn't hungry after all. It was amazing what idle gossip was discussed in the staff canteen. It turned out that a rather handsome Dr John Stokes was engaged to be married. The staff joked that it would take some dedication to snag such a prize bull. Enraged and betrayed, Danni tried to end their linen room rendezvous, but when he looked at her from his large brown eyes, she just melted all over again. He said that he didn't love his rather well-connected fiancé and was just going along with it all to keep his parents happy, whether she was pregnant or not.

Danni settled into her love life and her circle of friends, but never the twain could meet. Jack had even sweet-talked Max into nurse training. She wasn't too sure about Daniel, though. Midwife or no midwife, something in her gut just didn't feel right. She had a vague recollection of him, but strangely, their paths had never crossed before.

Where the hell had Max gone? He had just disappeared into thin air without so much as a goodbye. They drove up to Max and Daniels's pad to find a load of vultures picking away at the bones to get a story. Jack and Danni sobbed as they watched the story unfold in the press. When she closed her eyes, she imagined him somewhere, anywhere, doing God knows what. It just didn't bear thinking about. And when he did thankfully return, all she wanted to do was to protect him. She knew that it was going to take every last drop of tenderness in her to restore Max's confidence.

It was lovely to see that Jack had finally found a little light relief within the beaded lashes of Miss Nancy Éclair. He was happy, and that was all that mattered to her. Danni was pleased as punch with her other work in progress too. To her absolute relief, Max had qualified as a nurse. And this spurred Danni on to see her old friend Sharron Varley, the sister in the neurosciences ward. Danni sat with Sharron in the chaos of her office, admiring her rugby player pin-up calendar. Sharron was livid when she heard how Max had been abused by staff at the hospital and said he would be safe in her experienced hands. Even Wayne, the new man in his life, seemed like a keeper. He was patient, kind, handsome, and deaf. The deaf part was a bonus. He was

Danni's secret weapon in a crowded pub because he could lip-read any conversation from afar. For some strange reason, the antics of one particular blonde-haired, domestic assistant who was no stranger to the Porter's Lodge were usually on the tip of everyone's tongue.

Danni couldn't pack up his life. That could all wait until she was ready to say goodbye. Instead, she lay on his bed, cuddling a pillow and inhaling his familiar scent. Through glassy eyes, she clocked his portable and remembered how he had publicly humiliated her over the TV reception, blaming the interference on the buzz of her lady's finger. If only she could hear him laugh for one last time.

Jolted back into the chapel by the sound of Max's stifled cry, Danni decided to do what she did best and prop everyone else up. There was no way that she was going to lose anyone else.

Chapter Eighteen

The neglect reminded me of a holiday park that had been derelict since the nineteen seventies. It was all 'Hi-de-Low' with not even a smidgeon of 'Hi-de-Hi' in this part of southwest London. The discovery of used condoms under our bed was about as welcoming as this rental flat got. Banging the bobbled sofa produced a mushroom cloud of dust and dead skin cells. I was rewarded with a former tenant's credit card statement, a half-chewed sweet and a handful of long greasy blonde hair when I slid my hand in between its sagging bottom. What had we done? No, what I meant was, what had I done? The nets hung like ancient shrouds at the filthy panes that hadn't been washed since the nineteen thirties. Tasting mildew, I wobbled, dropped my stiff upper lip and sobbed. Why had I made this pig-headed decision so quickly?

Streets were lined with yesterday's chip papers rather than gold. Relentless roars of traffic and exhaust fumes are just too much. Where once there was cosmopolitan beauty, now there was just functionality. Trying to put on a brave face, I stared through the foggy window onto the central lawn. My gaze dribbled on the four floors of balconies that snaked around the building. I tried hard to picture an excited gaggle of flapper girls in fringed frenzy swishing by on their way to the latest jazz club. But in reality, it was as if the very soul of its cracked plaster had been ripped out. And here we were with bleach in hand with no choice but to scrub as if our lives depended upon it. There was no way we were moving into this filth until the stench of former inhabitants had been exorcised. Was this the price to pay for a Junior Charge Nurse post in the Neuroscience wing of a Large London teaching hospital? Did those navy blue epilates mean that much to me? Wayne had got a job at the same hospital as a health care support worker, three floors below me, which would lead to his nurse training. Cleaning the flat was the easy part, but learning to live like a Londoner was a whole new ball game.

And yet here we were, navigating the delights of public transport on our way to work. I missed the casualness of sauntering through the village on foot after a shift at the City Infirmary. The Tube lines were nothing short of irritating phlebitis. It was the kind of illness that crept up on you without warning, leaving you with delirium. In total bewilderment, we were pushed out of the way by the crowd of commuters as they travelled from one source of infection to the next. There was no time for kindness as we struggled to survive in this festering world. It was less mind the gap and more of a case of mind your sanity. I couldn't cope with being pressed up against total strangers in this game of twisted Twister.

Reminiscent of a stout, grey-haired Sybil Fawlty, Senior Sister Doris rose unsteadily from her thrown. She wore her navy-blue dress-like armour to fight off anyone who dared to step onto her tentacles. Her London accent hung in the air like stale fish as she slithered towards me. But she didn't scare or intimidate me. If anything, she needed me more than I needed her. She told me that she had been the sister in this neuroscience ward for three years now. Patting herself on the back, she explained that this was equivalent to a lifetime within the transitory world of London nursing. What would she think of the likes of Sister Dickson who had truly given her entire life to nursing? There was no point in having this conversation with Doris as she just wouldn't understand or even value this level of dedication.

Doris had the control of a runaway mine train. It was chaos, but not the kind of chaos that is funny. Staff were grimy headless chickens; to say that the uniform policy was stretched was an understatement. One male nurse caught my attention for all of the wrong reasons. As I got closer to say hello, I wanted to reach for an oxygen mask. Uniforms should be crisp, clean, and worn to project professional kindness. But this man needed bathing in sheep dip.

To my trained eye, the patients needed a dose of good old-fashioned nursing care too. I caught one of the nurses slapping a pot of tablets on a patient's bedside table without so much as a smile, let alone an explanation. She didn't even know if the patient was able to take them because she hadn't bothered to stop and ask. When I got closer to the patient's bedside, I saw an accumulated pot of tablets from an earlier medication round. I just couldn't help myself and jump in, there and then. Taking her to one side, I introduced myself politely and made it clear that I would not stand for this. What a way to make a first impression.

I couldn't be bothered to weigh Sister Doris up. Although smiling on the outside as we chatted, on the inside, I was screaming. There was so much to do and so much to change, but the first thing on my agenda was sitting smiling back at me. Danni was, of course, as always, my saviour. I spent hours ranting down the phone at her like some wailing banshee. Without her guidance and support, I would have had no idea of how to tackle the enormity of this ward. With her words ringing in my head, I decided that there was only one way to digest this animal; piece by piece. And the first to be eaten was Sister Doris herself.

My story is all about connection and people. It is not a nursing leadership theory textbook. These books have been done to death over the years by theorists who are far more experienced than me. Anyway, many of the leadership theories are regurgitated within the guise of the latest political fashions and fads. However, it would be naïve of me to not give some fleeting explanation of the framework on which we hung the ward rescue plan upon. Our rocky road to recovery was loosely based upon the pillars of clinical governance; clinical effectiveness, risk management, audit, staff management, education and training, information sharing and, of course, patient's voice at the centre. And before I send you to sleep, this is where my acknowledgement of theory begins and ends.

To my utter amazement, the team was behind me because they wanted things to improve as much as I did. It was really hard work but equally lots of fun as we soldiered on in our collective ambition to improve patient care and make the ward a nice place to work. My taste for nursing leadership was based upon doing the do and not just talking the talk. I led a team who came from all around the world and had vast experiences working within other healthcare structures. This cultural melting pot of inclusion fostered a vision where every-one's voice was equally heard and valued. We shaped things together, listened to each-other and respected our collective core values. Even if they did have to tell me to slow down when I spoke, because no one could understand my northern accent properly.

All that Tarak knew was searing agony. His pain had invaded every last cell of his body and was not letting go. But where was he? His stomach curdled like sour milk. What was that thing in his hand? It looked like some kind of dirty needle again. A thousand pneumatic drills penetrated his skull. Something soggy was wrapped around his temple. Was he still bleeding? Some sick bastard had shaved one side of his head whilst he had been out. Was this some kind of satanic ritual? He couldn't remember paying the Ferryman. Spluttering, he ran his cracked tongue over his lips. No, no Obol was hiding here. His broiled anus burned as if he had been relentlessly buggered by Satan himself before being passed around to all of his chief demons. Their collective cum still bubbled up inside him, waiting to explode. Gripping onto the metal rails that held him here, he then choked and vomited. His mouth was now being sucked out by a demon's pointed tongue. This monster guzzled and slurped on the taste of his vomit. Tarak wasn't going to give in to this hissing fucker so easily. But as there was now more than one of them to fight off, it was completely useless. And with that, he slipped back into unconsciousness, waiting for the next bout of terror.

"Tarak, it's ok, you are in hospital, you are safe now. My name is Max. I am a nurse, and I want to help you."

This poor soul thrashed against the bed frame in terror. He pushed away the plastic suction catheter that I used to stop him from aspirating on his vomit. Try as I might, no amount of reassurance could stop him from picking at the wound under his bandage as he came to. John worried when Tarak didn't return after his trick. He stepped through the bins that spewed rubbish into the alleyway, careful not to disturb his friends who may be shooting up. And who could blame them? Anything to provide a moment of relief from this. The familiar rustle of vermin gnawed on anything that lay still for too long. But the stench of rat piss and rotten food wasn't the worse evil in this London back alley. Why was it taking Tarak longer than usual? John knew that there were some sick punters out there and he had the scars to prove it. Most wanted more than what they were willing to pay for. And on this frosty February night, Tarak's rapists just took what they wanted, anyway. He was just another dirty rent boy that needed to be taught a lesson. These filthy queers continued to breed like mice, no matter how much the gang tried to put them out of their misery. John found

Tarak's trembling body, covered in blood, spit, cum, and shit. He was alive; but only just.

Tarak escaped to London with the clothes he stood in and thirty pounds in his ripped back pocket. He was not going back into that children's home in Bradford for nothing or no one. He had no intention of being forced back to live with his birth family, either. His Uncle was a towering and respected member of the local community and he was just an invisible, lying nothing. But every cloud has a silver lining; at least Tarak was getting paid for his affection now. John held Tarak's hand as I carried out my neurological observations. For John, Tarak was his whole cardboard-flavoured world. Nothing else mattered as long as they were together. I could not return this juvenile couple to the streets to face God knows what again. Whilst the care system had failed these two young men, I would not. I spent hours and hours just slowly peeling the onion. I didn't judge or try to fix anything, I just listened. Eventually, they even agreed to accept help and support. I was so relieved that these two boys left my ward hand in and hand but into a place of safety.

Chapter Nineteen

Wayne and I had each other, but that was about it. Once we were bored of the tourist traps and sights of the capital, we became lonely. Everyone else had been left up north in my rush to go down south. But all of that was about to change one morning on the way to the rubbish bins. I nearly dropped the black plastic bag of last night's takeaway cartons in excitement. No, I hadn't imagined it, I had heard a friendly 'Hello' coming from two doors down. The only time that people normally smiled or even spoke to me was when my wallet was open. And then, they were only talking to the ten-pound notes. There was just no social chit-chat happening in this part of South West London. And yet, there she was, standing on her doorstep, smiling radiantly from ear to ear. Half bemused but extremely happy to be recognised as more than a wallet, I stopped and found myself smiling back in eager anticipation of striking up a conversation. Before we knew it, we were chatting like two old fishwives over a garden fence.

I was content to just go with the flow when she invited me in. I sat and took in my surroundings as Harley disappeared through a beaded curtain towards her small but perfectly formed kitchenette. An incense stick casually wafted its calmness around the painted earth tones and warm eclectic textures. Moments later, she appeared with an earthenware mug of tea. I noticed that she curled a finger in her mop of black hair that bobbed freely around her high cheekbones and hazel eyes. The more she cackled, then the more her hair danced. She confessed that she had clocked Wayne and me as we went out to work together. Putting two and two together, she had figured that she was probably safe. By now we were belly laughing as I said it was just a lucky coincidence that I had sent my axe to the ironmongers for sharpening only that morning. By the time the incense stick had burnt out, we realised that we had so much grit in common. She had given up everything to tread the boards and follow her heart. She left her home and job as a science teacher in the Black Country to complete her metamorphosis. We understood each other's quiet quest for acceptance in this mainstream world. Whether it was the Indian or gay culture, it did not matter, we were both marginalised. Harley's infectious laugh and perceptive sensitivity were just the tonic that I craved. We became hooked on both the front and backstage antics of her career, relishing every single grease-painted moment of it. Within this world, you could be anyone you wanted to be. One minute you could be a children's television presenter, the next you could be a Shakespearean actor and the very next you could be a famous soap actor. Everything and anything is possible in Harley's world with equal amounts of talent, dedication and hard work. But her world was strangely parallel to my professional life. We were both skilled at using the medium of connection to captivate our audience. Regardless of what was going on behind the scenes, we knew how to give a performance of a lifetime.

But without Harley, I am not sure how we would have got through the next few months of agony. Life changed on Christmas Day morning when the line between Wayne's reality and fantasy fell. He couldn't move, he couldn't speak, and he couldn't escape this crippling weight. And no amount of blue roses would rescue him from this inhospitable hell. It had taken a cardiac arrest for Wayne to shatter. It was his fault that the lady arrested and died; if only he had experienced nurses working with him. There may have been more chance of spotting that she was poorly beforehand. But no, the agency staff were as clueless as him. They didn't even know where to run for the cardiac arrest trolley. He scrambled aimlessly through bits of equipment, trying to locate a plastic airway and a re-breathe bag, determined to push some oxygen into her lifeless lungs. As he tilted her head backwards to get a good seal of the mask, her eyelids fell open. She was staring at him through fixed eyes that no amount of classroom training could have prepared him for. The other so-called nurses attempted cardiac compressions. Blood lunged from her mouth with every pound to her chest. Wayne's perfectly ironed white tunic was ruined. Her ribs cracked under the weight of their uncoordinated attempts at resuscitation. When the experienced cardiac arrest team did arrive, it was too late; the patient was dead. And yet she still stared.

In Wayne's eyes, it was his neglect that had killed her. He hovered over the tranquillizers on the side of the kitchen worktop, making pretty patterns as they fell. He swore blind to Max and the psychiatrist that he could be trusted with them. But then again, he was a master of deception when he needed to be. As his fingers came into focus, the woman's blood was still on his hands. The more he swirled, the more a childhood nursery rhyme rang in his head. Grandad Arthur had sung this melody to him whilst he was learning to speak. *Three blind mice, see how they run.* He wished he was back in the pub, curled up with him. But his Grandad was never quite the same after the explosion. Any loud noise seemed to set him off. He didn't even play his beloved piano. Life dwindled from him as quickly as the pub's customers. It was not safe there after the explosion. *They all ran after the Farmer's wife who cut off their tail with a carving knife. Did you ever see such a thing in your life as three blind mice?* But he wasn't singing alone.

Wayne hadn't clapped his eyes on this boy since their time together in the cellar, but he could still hear him speak. Now fully grown but still his double, the man shouted 'No, no, no' over and over again, getting louder as Wayne played with the tablets. And then there was silence as the clatter of a key turned in the door.

I was only sure of one thing. No career was worth seeing my beautiful man lying on the floor in the dark, curled in the foetal position and paddling in his own urine. He was talking to someone who just wasn't there. You didn't need to be a psychiatrist to see that this plan wasn't working. Even our night-time strolls alongside the Thames weren't helping anymore. It just didn't bear thinking about what could have happened. I had failed him and now understood why the caged bird sings. I gently bathed my broken man and put him to bed. At least, if nothing else, this was one thing that I knew how to do properly.

Where once had been rain, there was now a rainbow. I was much more of an attractive proposition back home and quickly got an interview. It was not just any old post either. Somehow I was shortlisted for a ward manager job at Eastfield community hospital. I imagined the ruffled reactions of the traditionalists back home. They wouldn't be happy, to say the least, if by some miracle I could pull this off. I heard the clatter of the roulette wheel spin again when I put my chips on red twenty. Jack's voice popped into my head and said,

"Just bloody go for it, Max. You do not need my epiphany in Tiffany pep talk anymore. I'll be sitting on your shoulder instead. You can do this."

God, how I missed him. If I was successful at the interview then I would be on equal pegging with the likes of Sister Dickson and Sister Sharron. Oh, the bloody hellfire.

I had never been to the Eastfield before. However, it was bizarrely welcoming and familiar. These Victorians must have had a cookie-cutter hospital design book. I wondered if both the City Infirmary and her cousin had visited the same expensive Parisian perfumery when on tour. I could see them giggling in all of their Victorian fineries as they swished through Gay Paris. Perhaps they had shared the same delicate crystal atomiser. Sitting outside the interview room, the top notes of decadent decay, the middle tones of hospec and the under notes of hospital food floated past. It was showtime. My black brogues squeaked along the highly polished parquet. What a way to make an entrance. I stumbled on a chair by an ornate focal fireplace. Whilst waiting for introductions, I clocked that those frugal Victorian builders must have ordered a job lot of ceramic tiles.

The interview panel consisted of two senior nurses and the hospital manager. I took an instant liking to them. You could tell that they had seen it, heard it, and done it all before. They playfully bantered with each other as if sitting on a bus on the way to the bingo. This was a far gentler world than the hardness of nursing down south. Shirley introduced herself as the hospital matron. From the moment she peered from behind her white-rimmed glasses and mop of greying golden hair, I could just tell that we were going to get on like a house on fire. Her kind eyes twinkled with a lifetime of nursing service, willing me to do well. She was more interested in my values and me as a person, rather than my professional responses.

And then it was Eunice's turn to chat with me. She sniggered like a naughty schoolgirl and told me that she was a new-fangled advanced nurse practitioner. She explained that this role had been developed to bridge the gap between the world of nursing and medical care. Whilst this completely piqued my interest, this wasn't the time and place to pick her brains. I was here for the job of ward manager and nothing else. Well, not yet at least, anyway. Eunice was as lovely as she was knowledgeable. Now and again she would flick back her auburn bob to ensure that I could see her encouraging smile as I raced through her interview questions. And then it was Jan's turn to question me. Although she was the hospital manager, she was also an experienced nurse by background. To be honest, I was not sure If I was at an interview or watching a cookery program. Jan was a dead ringer for a young Nigella Lawson. Hoping that my interview had left the right taste in their mouth, I swapped recipe cards and left.

I went back to London to await the panel's decision. Harley had kindly agreed to spend the day with Wayne whilst I had been gone. Wayne knew that I was trying to move heaven and high earth to get us home in one piece. Just as I was fumbling for the keys to get over the threshold, I heard the telephone ring. With no time for pleasantries, I dashed over to catch the receiver before it rang off. I had done it. I was to be the new ward manager within an older person's rehabilitation ward at Eastfield Community Hospital. We were moving back home, for good this time. It meant so much more to me than just a career transition. I just wanted my Wayne to get better. Harley did what she did best and hugged us.

My career had gone full circle. I had become the very thing that I had idolised for all of those years. All of those ward sister's juice had seeped into my psyche unconsciously, whether or not I wanted it to do so. I just couldn't imagine attending the same ward manager meetings as Sister Dickson or, indeed, Sister Body. But that was where the similarity would end. I would do things my way, with calm, kind compassion. In my ship, everyone would be equally welcome as we sailed the sea of authentic inclusivity together. Under my ward leadership, I vowed that no one would ever be excluded. We would celebrate our difference whilst putting the patient at the absolute centre of what we did together as a team.

I had ordered a block-coloured navy-blue tunic top and matching trousers. Uniforms were now ordered directly from the supplier. The uniform policy had been modernised since the days of the traditional ward manager attire. Luckily for me, the frilly pork pie hat and matching ruffles had long gone out of fashion. Gone was the need for a sewing room, too. Well, I guess that meant that Maggie wouldn't have to wear those latex gloves and aprons when measuring me up. I had heard on the grapevine that Mrs M had taken pity on her. Maggie found a job as a domestic assistant on the outside rota. I just hoped she understood what 'pm' actually stood for.

Wayne was doing so well. I saw my glistening man return to me. His own experiences of living with a mental health illness led him to a whole new career path. He too spun the interview roulette wheel and landed a job as a project manager within a charity that was focused on disability. With such empathic confidence and lived experience, he then moved on to work within the deaf community. We had firmly put our roots down and purchased a two-bedroomed semi. There was love from our pink palace again. Only this time, I appreciated it all so much more. Quite often I would come home to the dulcet laughter of Danni, Aunt Bren, or whoever was free from our circle of friends and family. Wayne loved a good chin wag and coffee. God knows what they chatted about whilst I was not around, though. Sometimes it is best not to know these things.

I needed to put my demons to bed. I pulled outside the City Infirmary and thought about all the highs and lows that had happened here. A million memories flooded my mind as I slowly sauntered through the revolving doors of her grand Victorian entrance. She was still as beautiful as the day that I had first clapped my eyes on her. But now I knew her well. She was capable of delivering both great kindness and great cruelty within the blink of her powdered eye.

I passed the entrance of many of the wards where I worked during the earlier part of my career. Peering through a plastic partition, I saw Sister Dickson still arranging the bedside tables in perfect perpendicular perfection. However, these days, it just took her a little longer. I caught the back of Aunt Bren jangle and then dutifully disappear into the porter's lodge. It was probably wise not to follow and disturb her. The names of the pottery owner benefactors who had generously given birth to the City Infirmary long before the conception of the NHS were still etched in ceramic magnificence above the ward doors for the whole world to see. I watched the much loved and revered orange-clad domestic assistant army wax and clean the underbelly of the hospital. The concrete thirty-nine steps to Heaven were still busy. I smiled to myself as I watched a flurry of student nurses hurry to their wards. I wondered which poor unfortunate soul had inherited my old room. It was just as well that those walls could not talk. Nothing had changed but also at the same time, everything had. As I glided over the black and white tiled square, I found myself silently saying 'thank you' over and over again until I reached my destination.

It still haunted me, malingering like toothache, chipping away at my confidence. The stench of hot fat hit me as I wandered down the blue greasy steps. It was now lunchtime, and the staff canteen was positively bursting to the seams with all and sundry. I wondered if I was going to be able to find a seat. Luckily it wasn't Fish Day Friday. That gut-wrenching smell hadn't left me after all. This time, I held my head up high as I walked through the heavy doors. I joined the queue and slowly sauntered past the food to a mumble of chatter. And then a miracle occurred. Not only did the canteen staff serve me, but they graciously let me use their cutlery. They even remembered to use my name as they passed my jacket potato and cheese over the hot counter.

The hairs on the back of my neck stood up. As I gazed over the Formica gravestones, I caught sight of the whole purpose of my visit. I slowly swished towards Carla and Vivien as they sat with their party of apes. It was priceless to see the look of shock and confusion when they saw my navy blue uniform. All of a sudden, I didn't feel angry anymore. If anything, I pitied them. I lingered for a second by an empty chair at their table, smiled and headed for the Sister's lounge instead. Jack would have found this hilarious. I sat down on the padded green chair and stared out. I noticed Sister Lowly and Sister Dickson were huddled in the corner, daintily drinking tea from bone china cups. They were engrossed in polite conversation and didn't even notice my arrival in their world. In reality, I hated this area. But for now, it had finally served its purpose. Who was I to break with such tradition, anyway?

Chapter Twenty

The scum from a thousand bodies lined the water's edge. God knows what was lurking at the bottom of the pool. Pulling myself out of the water was the easy part but deciding to dive was much trickier. Jack's voice echoed through my head as I walked the plank,

"You don't change, do you? Either jump or I will push you off myself. And as you know, I'm a master at falling off things."

I closed my eyes and landed in my office. Staff were expecting to see their new ward manager and not a dripping idiot. Eunice flung open the door and said,

"Welcome Max, it's great to see you. Shirley sends her apologies as your first week clashes with her holiday. She has taken her grandkids to a holiday park for the week. Rather her than me, give me three wards any day compared to that. I have told her that there is more chance of winning the Knobbly Knees than the Glamourous Granny but she won't have it. Gosh, look at me rambling on, sorry. Sit down and gather your thoughts. You look petrified. Don't worry, the team can't wait to meet you."

"Thank you, you are very kind," I replied.

"Just to warn you, the nurses have got you a present," she beamed back.

But whatever could this be? As we sipped tea and chatted, I began to relax and look around my office. A large beech desk complete with a keyboard and monitor was shoved in the corner, overlooking a view of trees and grass. Three hard plastic orange chairs were interlinked across the back wall; these things just bred like rabbits. A rusty filing cabinet sat in the corner of the room, waiting for Hong Kong Phooey to jump out at any given moment. Despite having the window open, a cheesy smell was coming from somewhere. The culprit turned out to be a pair of sloppy slippers under the desk; a leaving present from the previous ward manager.

Once the slippers were safely bagged and removed, we went to meet the team. My ward was set out as a 'split Nightingale' ward. To the left of the central T plan was a large men's dormitory and to the right was the lady's. Long arched cathedral windows punctuated each side of the ward. The central part of the junction housed a series of side rooms, bathrooms and a nurses' station. Although I had never stepped on the ward before, it was all vaguely familiar. Even the green checked counterpanes, the beige bedside chairs and the very smell of hospec were comforting. At any second, I thought that Sister Dickson would appear from behind the floral bedside curtains and start to plague me. But that was in another lifetime.

Eunice led the way into the gaggle of staff. Everything was so casual and informal here. There was no Doris the sea witch to contend with. After a while, even my left leg stopped shaking. Sally, the deputy ward manager, smiled from behind her gold half-frame glasses, flicked back her black bob and presented me with a cardboard box. Laughing, she said,

"I bet you thought we were nuts when we asked for your shoe size, didn't you? Well, the truth of the matter is that we've had a whip round. Don't be flattered, we do it for everyone."

I was thrust a box which contained a pair of canvas shoes. Before I had the chance to say thank you, she jumped in.

"Welcome to our 'Shh' project. We wear soft shoes at night to minimise the noise in the wards. We don't want you clumping around in the evening."

"How kind, who needs ruby slippers when I have got these blue pumps?"

But there was no need to click my heels. I was already home. The Eastwood crew were practising 'civility saves lives' long before it was a thing. This movement advocates that all excellence in healthcare is dependent on every team member having a voice. Civility between team members creates a sense of safety. Whilst incivility robs teams of their potential, causes stress and can become the catalyst for people to leave. My gut instincts were right. I had stumbled upon a great nursing team made up of decent people. We just changed things together. But despite my best efforts, there was just one nurse who dug her heels in the past.

Poppy had worked at the Eastwood for years and had a reputation for spitting out ward managers. And the last nine hours and twenty-two and a half minutes gave her time to chew over her attack. I never understood the precision with which a night shift was timed. It caused a monthly nightmare when signing off unsocial duty payments because I am rubbish at maths. It took a calculator, a lot of cursing, and a couple of paracetamol on the twenty-eighth of each month to work this conundrum out. Where was Carol Vorderman when you needed her? And the ward budget was a whole league of migraine in itself. Every line of the statement sheet was covered in code, and every code could be easily split into pay and non-pay. But all this paperwork could wait till after work. There was no way I was sitting in the office whilst my staff worked their fingers to the bone.

"You're nothing but a bully. What do you think you are doing, Max?" greeted me as I staggered into the early shift report.

"If I'm honest with you Poppy, I have no idea what you are on about. Let's chat, but not here."

Why on earth was this ample woman in a skin-tight staff nurse uniform and plunging neckline trying to intimidate me? Still going for the kill, she spat,

"Why have you sent letters to folk asking them to meet you for a sickness review? No one has done that before."

Right, now I understood, it was just a storm in a teacup. I was doing nothing more, nor nothing less than following policy and procedure. But she was right on one account. I had no idea why this hadn't been implemented before.

"Poppy, can we please take this discussion somewhere a little more private? Let's go to my office and clear this up before you go home. I don't want you to leave here angry or upset."

Once she was slumped into one of my office chairs, I piped up,

"Poppy, I would never bully anyone. You have hurt me. But I'm sorry if my predecessor didn't follow the sickness policy. It is on the shelf at the nursing station, along with every other one. Please spend some time familiarising yourself with it. Don't let things bubble up, I just want to help. It may be useful if you attend our clinical supervision group. I have put some of these on in the evening, as I know you work night shifts."

Despite my best efforts, I couldn't get through to her. Six months later, at three o'clock in the morning, I found out why. It wasn't unusual to get the odd out-of-hours phone call from staff. This came with the territory of taking twenty-four-hour responsibility for the ward. Wayne's vibrating alarm was going off as Pongo jumped up and licked my face awake. There is no better way to be welcomed into the land of the living than by Labrador wet kisses. Pongo wasn't a disability dog; he was just a stinky black-haired ball of affection, protection, and love. I grappled for the phone and croaked,

"Hello, Max speaking."

"Max, it's Poppy."

"Is everything OK on the ward? What is wrong?" I inquired.

"I'm not working tonight. I'm standing outside your Uncle Jonny's house. The police are here."

Poppy was blubbering down the phone. What had she been doing outside his house? How did she know him? And why the fuck was she phoning me about this in the middle of the night? And with that, I was wide awake.

Chapter Twenty-One

A spray of worn leather and fresh sweat followed him into the pub. Buckled black boots clanked as he strutted towards the bar like John Wayne without the horse. Taking off his helmet and throwing back his long black hair, he said,

"Come on Pidge, pour me a pint. I'm gasping after a hard day bricklaying."

"From what I hear Jonny, that is not the only thing that you have been laying lately. Talk about loving them and leaving them. Which poor girl's heart have you broken this time? It's a good job that you are my brother."

Bren passed him a pint and just managed to duck before he blew the froth at her again. Their laughter filled the air with a cross between a climaxing orangutan and a machine gun.

"Well, Bren, it takes one to know one. I have heard that you have had more pricks than that dart board over there,"

The bloody cheek of him, even if he did have a point. Bren jumped over the bar and spent the next five minutes chasing Jonny around the pub. The regulars laughed and jeered on like extras in this Benny Hill sketch. They were kids again, but in all honesty, their childhood memories were anything but fun.

Mrs Armitrudes clapped out Mini was struggling to cope with the twists in the conifer-lined gravel hill. She checked her auburn demi wave in the rear mirror whilst keeping one eye on her backseat passengers. Jonny and his two older sisters, Bren and Karen, sat huddled and crying on the cracked red leather. Nothing was standing in the way of date night in the Armitrude household. She almost tasted the Viennese slice on her tongue and felt the cork escape from a bottle of fizz. And if Cyril played his cards right, then she would even prise herself into her babydoll nightie. That always revved his engine, which is more than she could say about her Mini. A large double bay-fronted mansion sneaked out from around the corner.

Phew, once the three children were deposited, there was still time to slip out of her grey nylon twinset and into something far more comfortable when she got home. Maybe there was still time to find that black feather boa and tickle her husband's fancy, too. Yes, Mrs Armitrude couldn't wait to get home and unleash the beast that raged beneath her size twenty-four polyester. She just needed to drop off these snivelling children first. After all, it wasn't the first time that they had been here.

Jonny hated the kid's home, but at least he was out of arm's length of the belt. He didn't think that Baxter would miss a couple of mouthfuls of food. But Father caught him red-handed stealing the dog's food. It was just a pity that he couldn't run as fast as the whippet. Father shook his head like a rag doll before he landed on the linoleum. At least this time, there was no blood. Sid couldn't look after his children and his pox-ridden wife, too. He scratched his five o'clock shadow, packed his bag, and waited for the social worker to arrive. Life in his truck was better than putting up with this shit. Jesus Christ, how many times had Annie been admitted to the City Infirmary already with 'women's problems'? Jonny spewed all over the table. He would rather starve than eat this boiled cabbage and poached fish. It was no big deal. He could always find a lump of coal to chew on later.

It worked at home and always settled his stomach cramps. Bren and Karen jumped over a skipping rope, laughing for the first time in ages with the other girls outside. They caught him watching and waved him over. He had much better things to do.

Johnny clutched his head, cowered, and got into the bath. His makeshift traps had failed. There were strangers in his house. Do it Jonny, do it now, Jonny, do it before you are caught. You will go to prison if the police find out. And you don't like it in there. Remember what happened last time?

"No, no, no, go away. Fucking leave me alone. Please, please fuck off."

And then there was silence.

The police had gone when I arrived with Aunt Bren. I saw dry blood on the bottom of Poppy's dressing gown as she opened her front door. Just before my mother Karen and father Alan arrived, she wanted to get something off her chest. But why? I thought it was odd that she had her full face on at this ungodly time of night. I sat on her brown Draylon sofa as the story unfolded.

"There's no easy way to tell you this, but your Uncle Jonny is dead. I found him. The police have already removed his body from the scene. There's no foul play. You see, the thing is Max, he knew that I was coming over and would find him. I can't get that image of discovering him out of my mind. He was lying in the bathtub with black lips and dripping limp arms. His head had fallen backwards. He was staring at the ceiling. Blood was splattered everywhere. My footprints left a spongy soaked mess in the bathmat when I fell backwards. I nearly slid down the wall. I thought I was going to vomit over his mottled body.

"I knew that he was poorly and had been begging him for months to get some help, but he wouldn't. He said that people were after him. He wouldn't leave because he thought that the authorities were coming to lock him away again. I don't know if you know, but since his back injury in the eighties, he hadn't done a day's work. He was always quietly on the fiddle with one thing or another on the side and claiming benefits, too."

"Hang on a minute, are you telling me that you two were…"

"Yes, that is right, Max. And I took it all out on you. You see, in his eyes, I was only good for one thing and one thing only. I thought that maybe with patience and understanding, he would change."

"I don't know what to say, Poppy. My head is all over the place. So all this was going on before I started as a ward manager then?"

"You never stood a chance with me, Max. I hated you even before you even started. I am so sorry for everything. You look very similar to Jonny, and every time I saw you, my blood boiled."

It had been a long time since I had been so shocked. Just as I thought that things could not get any worse, my parents traipsed in. My Mother watched with interest when Aunt Bren threw her arms around me whilst my father made polite conversation.

I couldn't believe what I was seeing. To the malonic tones of Eva Cassidy's *Songbird* Jonny's teak coffin trundled down the central isle of St Michael's Church with a gun-shaped floral tribute on the lid. I knew that he had been a game-keeper in the past, but this was just terrible. As the coffin went past me, I looked to see if there was a matching razor blade made from white chrysanthemums with a trickle of red carnation blood. Even the vicar took a second glance as he stared down at the fiasco that was being wheeled towards him. Poppy took hold of my hand and smiled.

But with death comes new beginnings. The staff at work found it difficult to understand how Poppy had gone from a demon to an angel almost overnight. She became my right-hand woman in all of the ward developments. Eunice took me to one side and said,

"How in the name of all of the Saints have you managed to get Poppy on board, Max? Others have tried and failed for years, but for some strange reason, you have got through to her.

"Well, Eunice, let's just say that if I told you, then I would have to shoot you, so it is best not knowing"

And with that, we laughed on and got on with running a busy ward.

Chapter Twenty-Two

Like all good wards, there is always room for change. Sally, my deputy, was moving on to work in the community. A regular eight-to-four job was just easier to plan for around childcare. Shirley and Eunice called me over to their office to tell me their good news. I walked into a riot of schoolgirl giggles. Shirley's attempts at making a soggy bottom cake for the patients tasted more like a bottom and less like a cake. Keeping a straight face, I asked the two ladies how they knew what a bottom tasted like, soggy or otherwise. It took them a good twenty minutes to compose themselves. Every time they tried to be serious, they just laughed again. Finally, Shirley adjusted her white-rimmed glasses, ran her hand through her untidy perm, and tittered,

"Don't worry, Max, I have been in touch with the mothership. Until we can plug Sally's post properly, they are going to send us one of their foot soldiers. It will only be temporary until we can sort the job out and advertise it. But just before you go, can I ask your advice, please? What do you think of my chances with a spotted dick next time?"

I thought that Eunice was going to swallow her dentures or pass out. It took at least another hour before we were all ready for work again.

A couple of weeks later, Eunice brought Sally's replacement to the ward. Oh my god, what the bloody hell was Cara doing here? You could cut the atmosphere with a knife. Eunice looked uncomfortable and confused as she tried to introduce her to me.

"Eunice, we already know each other. Introductions aren't needed," I said.

"Er, well, I'll leave you to it then. I am needed on another ward," she said, then off she scuttled.

As Carla sat down, I noticed the crease of her navy-blue Junior Sisters uniform hung uncomfortably around her next. The collar of the stiff starched material was rubbing her neck.

"Well Carla, did you know that you were coming to my ward?"

"I am just doing as I am as told Max. I am about as happy to be here as you are having me. But to answer your question, I did know. I was told last week when your Matron requested some support".

Part of me wanted to hug her and tell her that everything would be fine, but I just couldn't. She scratched her collar and said that she even went to Danni for advice. Once her wooden parrots stopped shaking, she said that this would be a good thing for both of us. Whilst she did not doubt that we could be professional and work together, maybe it also was time to bury old hatchets and move on. It now made sense why Danni hadn't popped around over the last week. I thought she was just busy being Danni the champion of the World, turning out decent student nurses. Wait till I saw her. It was going to take at least a few pints in the Potters to make sense of all of this. It was time for a taste of Carla's own medicine. My nostrils flared and whilst looking at her directly in the eyes, I said,

"Just let me tell you, in your career, you will see all sorts of practice, but I will show you how to do things properly. This will form part of your nursing leadership bag whilst you are working in my ward. But let's make one thing clear: bent spanners just don't work. My tools have universal use that can be adjusted to wrap around the patients' and nurses' individual needs. With me, one size does not fit all."

"Well thank you, Max. I feel so much better for your words of wisdom. But you never gave me the chance to explain or even apologise, did you? As usual, you are all me, me, me. Can you remember that night in A and E when you snubbed me? And that trick you pulled in the staff canteen just shows me that you haven't changed one bit. You thought you were so clever when you disappeared into the Sister's Lounge, didn't you? But let me tell you something. Vivien and I were laughing at your childishness. How dare you sit there, holier than thou, and try to give me, of all people, a lecture on inclusive leadership and kindness? And you think it is clever to twist my advice too. Do me a favour and get over yourself, you bloody hypocrite. Can you remember Sadie from the oncology ward? That was my mother."

For once, Max couldn't find the words. But sometimes more is spoken in silent tears.

Although girdled up to the gods and plucked to perfection for a night at work, Sadie always put her family first. Whilst she mixed with the stars, nothing or no one was more important than Carla and her older brother, Darren. In her Norman Norell knockoff, shiny blonde bob and war paint, she could give Cilla a run for her money on any night of the week. It was just a pity that she hadn't got her voice, though.

"What's the matter with you, Chuck? Wipe those tears from your face and tell me all about it. Come sit with me whilst I throw on my make-up and get ready. I've always had a lorra lorra time for you. You treat Bobby and me like royalty when we are in town."

"Oh Cilla, you haven't time for this, you're on in 15 minutes."

Cilla smiled, turned around from her dressing table mirror and said, "I've always got time for you. You are like family. Let the audience wait. It won't hurt them, will it, Chuck?"

Through her panda eyes, she explained that her Terry had found a lump in her left breast during his Friday night flurry on the nest. A mammogram and a few prods later confirmed that it was the 'C' word. The thought of chemotherapy, radiotherapy and a radical mastectomy was bad enough in themselves. But Sadie certainly wasn't going to miss her idol sing.

"You know what Sadie, I live for today because you don't know what is going to happen tomorrow. But whatever you need, Bobby and I are here."

Cilla touched up her mascara and gave Sadie one of the kinds of hugs that connects the soul. She winked, slapped on her stage smile and walked out waving to the audience.

"Now, ladies and gentlemen, I have decided to mix things up a bit and pick a very special song for our Sadie. This one's for you."

The floor vibrated, the audience cheered, and Cilla belted out *Love of the Loved* to her purple-lit audience. When she closed her eyes, Sadie heard Cilla's words echo in her mind as the chemotherapy caused through her veins. As if losing it wasn't bad enough in the first place, it even stung as she brushed her hair through. Sadie ran her hand over the radiotherapy burn and scar tissue and thought of Terry. With the cancer in remission, she was now free to become a wife, mother, and confidant to the stars again. She didn't blame his infidelity either. After all, Terry had always been a breast man.

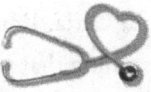

Max practised his floating table trick without even realising he was doing it. At any other time, this would have been funny, but not now and not tonight. Danni moved all three pints from the pub table before they were on the floor. Looking at him directly through pierced eyes, she said,

"I didn't tell you about Carla because I think this is a good thing for you both. There, I've said it, it's out in the open. You would have done anything to stop her from coming. You may have Shirley and Eunice wrapped around your little finger, but you can't charm me. And Wayne didn't know either, so you can leave him out of this."

Danni had not lost her edge. If anything, it was sharper. She could still stop me dead in my tracks if she wanted to.

"You're both right. Wayne, I'm sorry for being in a mood with you when I came home earlier. Danni, I'm sorry for blaming you for not telling me. Maybe you are right."

Danni smiled, curled her top lip, adjusted her red rims and replied, "Well, it's probably just as well that you have finally seen sense because I've asked Carla to join us. And I don't want a replay of handbags at dawn. To use your own words, Max, 'everything looks better after a few pints', so suck it up and play nicely or I will bang your heads together."

And there she stood in faded denim glory, a pair of white stilettoes and perhaps the curliest perm I had ever seen. Why did I have the urge to sing *Total Eclipse of the Heart* all of a sudden? Resisting the temptation to use my glass as a microphone, I smiled and waved her over. I put my hand on her thigh as she squished in and said,

"It's so good to see you, Carla. I'm so sorry that I have been such a pain. I deserve everything that you said. I've missed you."

"But I went too far. When Danni got on the phone earlier and brought me up to speed, I wanted to boil my head. And I have missed you too," she replied.

It didn't take long before we were cackling together. She had split up with her boyfriend and found herself footloose and fancy-free again. Now she wanted the kind of man who could shag her senseless on the living room floor but would also open the door for her. Carla wanted to still feel his stubble burn on her skin the next day. And she wasn't fussed about where this fantasy rash would appear, as long as she could walk. But there were slim pickings as we looked around the pub. In all honesty, she had more chance of platting snot.

Carla stood in the middle of our ward and waited patiently for Dr Lock to arrive. Although she looked like she had glided off a runway, this consultant geriatrician was no dumb blonde. Her exacting standards were as sharp as her wit and passion for patient care. But Carla could handle herself, even when faced with the most stubborn of doctors. Shirley and I watched her from behind the nurse's station greet a stream of visitors to the ward. A greasy-haired lady in her sixties, wearing a dirty red anorak, tapped Carla on the shoulder. She rustled in her plastic bag, found a pair of pink-rimmed glasses, and smiled through the crack of her nicotine-stained front teeth. Sadly, she didn't get the chance to speak as Carla jumped in, rubbed the lady's lower arm and said,

"Goodness me, you are perishing, my lovely. Did you come up on one of those drafty old buses that go around the reeking to just get from A to B? Let me get you a warm drink whilst we find your husband's bed. What is his name, darling?"

I thought that I was going to wet myself, pass out or both. Shirley nearly fell off the swivel chair. Our plan just couldn't have gone any better if we had tried. Droplets of spit spurted from the lady's mouth as she bellowed,

"I'm Dr Lock, not a bloody relative. I'm here to do my ward round."

Carla waited for the ground to open up and swallow her. The consultant tutted and huffed at Carla, stomped over to the notes trolley and took out a stethoscope from her crumpled carrier bag. Like jumping out of a birthday cake, we appeared as if by magic. Still tittering, Shirley said,

"Welcome to the Eastfield, you are one of us now. I think that Dr Lock is waiting to start her ward round. Get to it Carla, we mustn't keep her waiting."

Although still red, and scurrying off to apologise to the real Dr Lock, she turned and said,

"I'll get you my pretties and your little dog too."

But every cloud has a silver lining. Just before starting her game of granny bingo, as she called it, our consultant introduced a new junior doctor to our motley crew. Christian had flown in from the City Infirmary for a stint in older people's rehabilitation. For some reason, my mind wandered to Sharron Varley's office, and in particular, her rugby calendar. Christian was Mr January to December rolled into one bicep-bulging white coat. His chopped brown hair framed a chiselled face and twinkling blue eyes. I thought that Shirley's glasses were going to steam up as we watched his thick thighs and perched buttocks swagger over to Carla. I winked at my accomplice and whispered,

"You don't get many of them in a pound, do you, Shirl?"

And then we were off again. Well, laughter is the best medicine.

Mary lay motionless on her bed, hoping no one would notice her. As far as she was concerned, she was in Eastfield to die and that was that. It just wasn't the natural order of things; no one should outlive their children. Life had lost its sweet taste. She had fallen over and fractured her left hip. Following a hip replacement and detox at the City Infirmary, she was transferred to our ward for a period of rehabilitation. But you can only rehabilitate someone who wants to participate, and despite the team's best efforts, all this broken sparrow wanted to do was to wither away into the hospital sheets. Mary had been self-medicating with mother's ruin since the death of her daughter a couple of years ago. She swore blind to her carers and social worker that she had stopped drinking. But if nothing else, she was inventive. It was her legs that had stopped working and not her brain. And so she called taxi drivers to do her bidding, hiding her gin in the toilet cistern, away from prying busybodies.

The death of one baby in childbirth is more than enough to live with for any parent but losing another child was just impossible. If only she hadn't turned her back on her daughter when she needed her the most. At the age of forty-six, Pam had also decided that life had lost its sweet taste. With a pestle and mortar, she ground her late husband's stockpiled morphine tablets into a fine powder, mixed it with yoghurt and took her last supper.

Vulnerable and lonely, she welcomed the charming door-to-door salesman with American accents over her threshold. It was easy pickings to sell their brand of religion to someone who was already looking for belonging. It wasn't long before Pam was brainwashed, bled dry and dead. These black-suited vampires' religion was just not compatible with her mother's strong catholic faith. Pam gagged on the last spoon and stopped breathing. Maybe this was something she would chew over with God directly if she ever got there. Otherwise, she would be warm by the fire. Either way, anything was better than this.

There wasn't a dry eye on the ward round when the team learnt of Mary's predicament. Dr Lock moved swiftly because, as always, she only wanted the best for her patients. With Mary's consent, it took our consultant one phone call to her psychiatrist friend to arrange Mary's transfer to mental health services. It is useless trying to treat the body and neglect the mind. Conversely, this argument works in reverse. Any assessment must treat the patient's need as a whole. This must take into consideration the physical, mental, social, environmental, and spiritual aspects of a person's sense of being. It is ludicrous to break a person down into neat boxes, as human beings are far more complex than that.

Christian and Carla walked through Queen's Park, trying desperately to make small talk. First dates are always a bit awkward at the best of times. Carla bounced along in a pair of white figure-hugging jeans and a striped blue and white off-the-shoulder top. Luckily, she had chosen a pair of blue pumps, rather than her signature heals. If there was a next time, she would even flatten down her mass of curls too. Towering over her very own Tom Cruise with a shaggy perm and heels was not a good look. And anyway, Christian didn't need a creak in his neck. They stopped at an old bench opposite the bandstand as the scent of fuchsia-filled beds wafted in the evening air. Queen Victoria didn't bat an eyelid through her turquoise eyes; she had seen it all before over the years and was still definitely not amused.

Words just left his head if he looked into Carla's green eyes for more than a couple of seconds. He was still in shock that this goddess had agreed to go on a date with him in the first place. As well as being a great nurse, the woman sitting next to him was drop-dead gorgeous. He huffed, fidgeted, and finally got out,

"S-so, how do you know Max then? You two seem close."

Carla giggled and explained, "We've known each other for years, on and off. I encouraged him into nursing in the first place. He was nothing before he met me."

Now feeling a little more relaxed, Christian replied, "Well, you have certainly done a good job. He is a chip off the old block, isn't he?"

That was a backhanded compliment if Carla had ever heard one, but at least he was trying. Shuffling a little closer to Christian, she said, "Well, to be honest, I can't take all of the credit. His friend Danni has done the lion's share of the work and not to mention Wayne, his partner. But it was Jack who pushed him into student nurse training. That dastardly duo were inseparable; everyone thought that they were an item because they were so close. It completely floored Max when he died. He doesn't say anything, but he has never been quite the same since."

"I'm sorry to hear about Jack. I have a brother named Jack too, but sadly, I haven't seen him for years."

Carla looked at the longing in Christian's blue eyes and inched even closer. A fresh mixture of manliness, aftershave, and regret tantalised her senses. And he didn't even realise how attractive his gym-ripped body was. Christian needed to get something off his chest, and she was more than happy to sit there and soak him up. The mention of the name Jack brought all sorts of emotions to the surface. As much as he pleaded, they just wouldn't tell him why the black sheep of the family had been banished. One minute, his brother was in the middle of his RAF training and the next, he had vanished without a trace. What had Jack done that was so wrong? Even the RAF base wouldn't provide a forwarding address or contact number.

"Hang on a minute, your name is Christian Taylor, so am I right in thinking that your brother was Jack Taylor, then?" Carla asked.

"Yes, but what do you mean 'was'?" Christian replied.

Any appetite to play hide the popcorn in the back row of the flicks fizzled away. Instead, Carla gripped her date's hand tightly as she tried to camouflage her shock.

"I don't want to get any of this wrong, Christian, because I wasn't around for some of it. But if I am right, you deserve to hear the truth from the horse's mouth. Let me make a few phone calls."

"But what do you mean Carla? What is going on?" he asked, looking like a rabbit in the headlights.

Once out of the phone box, the couple made their way through Queens Park, onto the bus and into our home. Pongo was waiting, bushy-tailed and twice as daft as usual. When the door opened, he panted, knocked Christian over, and proceeded to lick him to death. There was no stopping this lovely lump of a labrador when the mood took him. Eventually Christian appeared from the floor, covered in dog slobber and black hair but smiling. I waved the couple to the kitchen while trying to grip Pongo's collar before he lunged again. As nice as it was, there was just no room to seat five people and a smelly dog comfortably in our living room. Wayne may have lovingly styled our lounge shabby chic, but it was no French Chateau. They just didn't make new houses with decent-sized rooms anymore. When our reclining chairs were fully extended, we could even turn on our TV with a toe.

Still wiping dog hair off his T-shirt, Christian stepped into the kitchen and sat down at a pine table. I felt the hairs on the back of my neck stand up. I burped, apologised, and said,

"Please don't be mad at Carla. I told her to keep quiet until you got here. I'm sorry. I don't know where to begin with all of this."

I could see the veins in his temples throb as he blurted, "Begin with what, Max? Please tell me what is going on, for Christ's sake. One minute I'm on a date with Carla and the next I'm here. Will someone please tell me what all this is about? What do you know about Jack? Is he OK?

There's no easy way to say this Christian, your brother is dead. And I'm so sorry to be so blunt, but you need to know the truth."

It started with his quivered lip but soon ran into a trickle of tears. He played with Pongo's velvet ears in silence for a while, until saying,

"So how do you know this? Were you close to my brother, then?"

"Yes, we were very close. I loved him with all of my heart. There isn't a day that goes by that I don't miss him. You look just like him. Sit for a while and when you are ready, we will try and help to make sense of this mess together."

Carla put her arm around her broken young man. Through equal amounts of laughter and tears, we all tried our best to fill in the missing pieces. We wanted to tell him so much, but it was a little like trying to pour the Atlantic Ocean into a thimble. And how could we possibly make Christian feel better? He had been robbed of too much already.

"But did he ever talk about me or our parents?" he asked.

Danni sighed, poured another round of tea, and admitted that she caught Jack crying into his pillow one night. He had reached out to his parents a few times, but they were not having any of it. He secretly hoped that his father would thaw, but this never happened. Jack even hung around the oncology ward door, wanting to get a glimpse of his dad. But Dr Taylor, our infamous oncologist, looked through him and carried on walking. It was just easier to leave the hospital for a new life on top of the bar of the European. Dr Taylor wasn't aware that Danni knew his dirty truth and chose to smile at him at his son's funeral. This wasn't the time or place to out him. She grabbed hold of Christian's hand, slurped her tea, and carried on. Christian went to London to complete his medical training. Whilst at arm's length from each other, the two brothers couldn't meet. And by the time Christian was back from the big city, Jack was conveniently dead, so the dots could never be joined.

On the outside, I was smiling, but on the inside, I was screaming, 'Who made you God all of a sudden?' But then again, I should've known better. It wasn't the first time that she had held her cards this close to her chest. She caught my eyes, and I quickly looked away before saying something that I couldn't take back. Sensing my hurt, Wayne grabbed my thigh under the table and anchored me before I set off into Storm Danni. And it worked, well, for now at least.

Christian looked like he had seen a ghost, so I passed him another biscuit. We didn't want him distraught and hypoglycaemic, too. He explained that as much as they tried, his parents couldn't hide the fact that they hated each other. It would have been far easier for everyone if they had divorced, but Maria, his mother, was far more interested in what the neighbours would say. A respectable bank manager does not get her dirty washing out in public.

"So you are telling me that Maria Taylor, the bank manager, is your mother? And she is married to Dr Taylor, our oncologist? Have I got that right in my head?" I said, almost choking on a custard cream.

"Yes, why? Is there something else I need to know?"

"Well, the bloody hell fire. But no, it's nothing bad. I just had no idea that she is your mother. Jack kept that one quiet too."

After all of this high drama, it was great to see Christian laugh. He thought it was hilarious how I had tricked his mother into giving me my first mortgage by 'butching it up'.

And when the dust settled and our unexpected guests had finally left, it was time to take off my nurse's smile and sob into Wayne's arms. Half angry and half confused, I looked up from his chest and said,

"How could Danni do that? She didn't have the right to keep it from me. I could've helped Jack if I'd known."

"Babe, she must have had her reasons, so just let sleeping dogs lie. Let's be real, she wouldn't do anything to willingly hurt you. Danni loves you. I know that you are hurt, but please let this one go. Not everyone needs to know everything, remember?"

"Yes, you are right. I'm still wondering why Jack didn't tell me who his parents were, though. But you are right, that donkey must have had his reasons too."

And with that, we cuddled up with Pongo on the sofa and fell asleep.

Chapter Twenty-Three

An explosion of glitter and laughter echoed from the corner of the dayroom. As I said hello and pulled up a pew, the group of ladies continued to mee-maw over Donny Osmond. They waved and mouthed 'Hello Max' over the clatter of ward life. The group seemed happy enough sticking and giggling, cutting and gossiping, embossing and chatting on their production line. The table was knee-deep in paper roses and red hearts, gold mirror board and cream cards. I was impressed by the speed at which this crimplene conveyor belt was churning out wedding stationery. Years of working in heavy industry were certainly being put to good use. Cindy, our ward diversional therapist and Carla sat in the middle of the belt, doing their best to supervise the frivolity.

"Watch yourself, Joan, if you are not careful, you are going to get your hearing aid stuck in the glue," Sylvia piped up.

"Right you are Joan. It's been years since I've had such fun. All of this is taking me back to my wedding," she replied, whilst carefully removing an embossed heart from her ear lobe.

"What do you mean Duck?" her friend asked.

"Well, I'll never forget that day as long as I live. There I was, gliding down the aisle looking like a vision in white lace and expectation. I wondered why the congregation were tittering to themselves as I got closer to my Cyril?"

By now, the whole production line had stopped for a tea break and was avidly listening to Joan's wedding day wonders.

"Well, go on, don't leave us girls in suspense Duck. What were they laughing at?" Sylvia asked.

"When I got to the altar and saw my Cyril, I lifted my veil and shouted, 'What the bloody hell have you done now?' at the top of my voice. My wedding photos were ruined."

"But why? Put us out of our misery?"

"Well, Sylvia, the bloody fool, had been out the night before, got drunk as a monkey, slipped on the ice and woke up with a filthy shiner. He looked like Quasimodo when I turned to say my 'I do's' in front of Father Simpson. I don't think that the poor catholic priest had heard a bride swear at the altar before. What a way to start a marriage."

The table shook with laughter and a thousand paper hearts floated into the air like confetti.

"What a shock. But let's hope that Carla has a better honeymoon than mine. My Alf and I scrimped and saved for a couple of nights in a B and B in Blackpool. But just between us girls, he left me high and dry on our honeymoon night," Sylvia revealed whilst simultaneously picking the paper out of her tea.

Joan raised her eyebrows and said, "You mean he didn't know how to operate his meat and two veg?"

"Imagine the scene. There I was, lying seductively spread eagle on the altar of sacrifice, almost fizzing with passion from underneath my pink nylon nightie," Sylvia explained.

"And what happened next, did you, er, well, become a woman?" Joan asked, whilst leaning in a little closer.

Sylvia explained, "Well you see, he got into bed, slithered his rough hand under my nightie and..."

"And what Sylvia? What happened?"

"I knew he had had one pint too many in the Flying Dutchman. He just, you know..." she said while picking up a strip of paper and letting it curl over.

"You mean he had brewers droop?"

"Yes, he had got himself into such a state about the whole thing that he just passed out. Instead of being de-flowered, I spent the night listening to him snore through his fish and chip-infused breath."

The group of women cackled as Sylvia bounced her perm with the palm of her hand and explained that all had not been wasted as her husband spent a lifetime making up for their wedding night. Well, they couldn't afford a television set and it was certainly cheaper than going to the flicks. Who needed the *Sound of Music* when her Alf could make her sing louder than Julie Andrews on any night of the week? Once he had found what his nether regions were for, the man was insatiable.

"Well, ladies, I'll be off and leave you to your girl talk before you embarrass me any further," I said, walking off laughing.

It was lovely that the patients were being roped into Carla's and Christian's wedding preparation. After all, this was the place where they had first clapped eyes on each other.

The taste of T-bone steak, eggs and those fancy croquet potatoes still lingered on Christian's breath as his mother poured him another glass of wine to wash it all down. Carla settled for a sensible Caesar salad instead. Nothing or no one was coming in between Carla and her wedding dress. Max and Wayne had spent too many agonising hours with her in every bridal shop from Lands' End to John O Groats to find the perfect dress for one unaccounted calorie to ruin things now. Dr Taylor senior. fumbled through the sweet menu with his wife until they both finally settled on the cheese board. An elderly waitress in a frilly white hat, black pinafore and white apron returned with another bottle of wine, an Irish coffee for Mrs Taylor, a selection of cheese and perhaps the biggest Knickerbocker glory that Carla had ever seen. From the safety of her melon balls, Carla watched her fiancé demolish the ice cream without spilling a single drop on the green tablecloth. This restaurant was just too sophisticated for any seepage or spillage. They certainly weren't in the staff canteen now.

Mrs Taylor was almost fawning over Carla from the other side of the table. From the moment that Christian had told his parents that they were tying the knot, she had been on cloud nine with open arms and chequebook. After all, only the best was good enough for her son and his blushing bride. Taking another gulp of wine, she patted her husband's hand, looked at Carla and said,

"I have been waiting for this day since my wonderful son was a little boy. We are going to have the biggest wedding since Prince Charles and Lady Diane. Now tell me again about the order of service. What music have you decided on, my darling?"

"Well, Mrs Taylor..." Carla tried to say, before being interrupted.

"No, Not Mrs Taylor, Carla, I have told you, please call me Mum. You're like a daughter to me."

"Well, Mum, we have decided on the village church near the City Infirmary. We both love that little chapel and it is so convenient for our friends and family too. I'm just hoping that there is enough room to get out of the wedding car in one piece and up those steps without flagging down the number twenty-three bus with my trail. I'm sure my bridesmaids will help me out, though. Oh, we have decided on *All Things Bright and Beautiful* for our first hymn. It is so uplifting, and we love the sentiment behind the words. Father Gregson will be officiating the service, as he is such a kind chap."

"Well, that sounds just perfect. I have not been there before, but I hear it is absolutely charming. George, you must know the church in your line of work?"

Dr Taylor blinked and said, "Yes, Maria, I do know the chapel. You are right, my dear. Sadly, I have attended many patient funerals there over the years. It's so sad when we lose one of them, it still gets me every single time."

Carla explained that every time she thought about Queen's Park, she could smell the heavy scent of fuchsia flowers hanging in her mind's eye. It only seemed natural that these should feature in her bridal bouquet and central table displays. Mrs Taylor, or Mum as she preferred, insisted on paying for their wedding reception. Well, if the University Grand Hall had been good enough for George's graduation ball and their wedding reception, then it certainly cut the mustard for their only son and his bride-to-be. Nothing could be better than a honeymoon in Majorca, either. If memory served her right, the family had spent many a happy hour there together when Christian was younger. If she played her cards right, it wouldn't be too long before Maria heard the pitter-patter of her grandchildren's feet on her Minton tiles.

Mrs Taylor called the waiter over, settled the bill, left a hefty tip, and linked her husband's arm before bidding goodnight to all of the patrons at their favourite restaurant. She gave her son and bride-to-be a hug and disappeared into the back of a taxi with her husband before her fake fur attracted the local stray cats. Once the coast was clear, Carla and Christian sat on a wooden picnic bench in the moonlight, hand in hand. Squeezing her hand, Christian looked at his beautiful wife-to-be and said,

"Thank you so much for going through with all of that pantomime. They are clueless, but I don't want to hurt them."

Carla leaned over the table, kissed him, and said, "Yes, I know. It's only the truth if it doesn't hurt, isn't it? I love you too much to burst their bubble."

Carla looked stunning. Her strapless diamante embroidered bodice gripped her torso before flailing out into a fishtail lace trail. She had opted for a simple silver taira and a pair of flat ballerina satin pumps to complement the look. A bouquet of white roses and pink fuchsia bells hung on her arm. It was such a privilege that she asked me to give her away. Her mother had passed of cancer and her father was, not to put too much of a fine point on it, missing in action. There wasn't a dry eye in the house as Wagner's wedding march serenaded us to the altar. The whole of the hospital's glitterati had turned out in their finest dip and tucker to celebrate the union of junior Dr Christian Taylor and junior sister Carla Jones. Father Gregson was beaming at the front of the church as I handed her over to Christian and collapsed in the front row next to Wayne. Christian looked handsome in a grey frock coat, crisp white shirt, and pink cravat.

Father Gregson looked over the congregation and said,

"Welcome to each and every one of you to God's home as we celebrate the love of two people. You are all equally welcome here. Before we start with the official order of service, Carla and Christian want to break with tradition and have asked me to play a song to remember anyone who couldn't be here today."

And with that Dolly Parton's *Islands in the Stream* drifted over the congregation. Once the ' till death us do part' bit was over, staff lined the path and formed an arch of bottles and bedpans outside of the church to welcome Mrs and Mrs Taylor to the world. Before getting into the wedding car, Carla turned around and tossed her bride's bouquet. I just didn't expect Wayne to catch it. He looked at me, laughed, raised his eyebrows and shrugged his shoulders. God only knew what was going through his head. I learnt that sometimes it is better not to ask.

Anyone who was anyone was there. Gaggles of nurses and doctors lined the ballroom, waiting for the happy couple to make their grand entrance. Multicoloured spotlights bounced off the central glitter ball, casting magic across the parquet floor. I caught Sister Body's eye, raised my glass and smiled at her. It was so lovely to see her have fun. Even Sister Dickson had made the effort to attend. She sat chit-chatting in a navy velvet dress with Dr Stokes and his wife and children. I grabbed hold of Danni's hand, squeezed it, and whispered in her ear,

"You've had a lucky escape. Have you seen him these days? He looks like the wild man of Borneo. Hasn't he let himself go? You can do far better than that."

She sniggered and said, "I know, he has put so much weight on. And look at the state of his wife. They are a pair together. Has that woman not heard of those lift and separate bras? Her boobs are flapping around like two wet udders in that cerise twin piece."

"Yes, I know, they are less cross your heart and more cross your knees. If she put a duster on the end of each nipple, she would be able to clean the floor."

On the other hand, Danni looked stunning in a figure-hugging black cocktail dress and matching bolero jacket. I noticed that the tips of her spikes looked even blonder than usual. Just as we were sharpening our claws for round two, the floor vibrated and the Master of Ceremonies told us to put our hands together and welcome Mr and Mrs Taylor to the dance floor. How rude, Danni and I were just getting started.

The happy couple looked beautiful together as they glided towards the centre of the dance floor. My mind wandered back to the first time I had clapped my eyes on Carla in the staff smoking room. There had been so much water passed under the bridge since then, but our relationship was stronger for all of it, warts and all. With the main lights turned down, it could have been Jack instead of Christian holding her. I tapped Danni on the shoulder and asked her for a tissue. I wasn't going to ruin my waistcoat and remove the dress handkerchief for love nor money. Wayne's hand slid past mine and grabbed my little finger as we waited for their first dance. As the speakers cracked, Carla put her hands around her groom's neck and moved in closer. They slow danced around the floor together, lost in a world of love and Cilla Black's *You're my World*. They stared into each other's eyes, singing the lyrics, oblivious to anyone around them. I could almost see Sadie standing with us. It was just beautiful.

Cheap toilet blocks couldn't mask the stench of pee that overflowed from the communal urinal. Trying not to breathe, I put one hand on the wall and let the last two pints of beer gush down the cracked enamel. The harsh fluorescent lights stung my eyes as I checked myself in the mirror. Whilst trying to get the paper towel dispenser to relinquish its grip long enough to dry my hands, I heard an odd noise coming from somewhere in the cubicles. Having deducted it wasn't the fizz of the electric fly trap or the gurgle of the drains. I crept from cubicle to cubicle, knocking on each one and asking if everyone was all right. One of the doors opposite the urinal swung open. Never in my wildest dreams did I expect to see Dr George Taylor sitting fully dressed, blubbering and bent over the pan.

"Dr Taylor, whatever is the matter with you? Are you unwell? Do you need some help? Shall I go and get your wife?"

"No, leave Maria out of this. It is nothing to do with her. I'm not sick. Please leave me alone."

"I'm so sorry Dr Taylor, I'm not going anywhere until I know that you are ok. It must be emotional to see your son get married, is that it?"

He got up from the seat and wiped his tears away. Staggering over to the sink and splashing cold water on his sallow face, he said,

"Thank you, Max, that will be all."

"Right Dr Taylor, let's make one thing clear. We are not at work now so you can't boss me about. I'll tell you what. Let me get you a glass of water and we can get some fresh air together. You may feel better after that," I insisted.

"Very well, if that makes you happy", he said, appearing a little more reasonable.

I returned a few minutes later and escorted him through the mock gothic foyer and into the gardens. He didn't seem to mind when I placed my hand on the small of his back to guide him to a bench overlooking a lake. This was a peaceful location as any to sober up. Weddings can be overwhelming for even the stiffest lip. His eyes twinkled when I told him that I preferred funerals to weddings, as at least I was guaranteed one of those. We sat for a while until he turned, looked at me directly in my eyes and said,

"You are very kind, Max, I mean that. I know who you are."

"Don't worry about it, you are welcome. I won't breathe a word of this to a living soul. I wouldn't want you to lose any face at your son's wedding. We'll make this our little secret, shall we?" I said, gripping his hand and leading him back into the foyer before anyone noticed that he had been gone for too long.

Chapter Twenty-Four

The new grey suit, silver-rimmed glasses, crisp white shirt and rainbow flag-inspired tie were the perfect combination to mark this occasion. But what had happened to my beautiful brown quiff and, more to the point, where had all of these wrinkles sprang from? I stood at the side of the stage waiting to go on and texted Wayne back. Bless him. After twenty-odd years of putting up with me, he knew just how important this speech was. Who would have thought that our mortuary brief encounter would have led to all of this?

Looking like Hinge and Bracket on a bad day, Aunt Bren and Danni discussed the price of butter at a carousel table at the front of the large auditorium. What was Danni wearing? Those TV shopping presenters could sell a bag of poo and make it look attractive. Just because something is on a special buy doesn't mean that you necessarily need it. You couldn't see the work surfaces in her kitchen for the menagerie of must-have gadgets. The kitchen was her Malc's domain, anyway. Danni had stumbled over him one night in the Potter's Arms, the poor bloke. Doesn't time pass quickly? To my reckoning, they had been together now for over fifteen years. He was a patient lump of a man who put up with her eccentricities. I suppose being a long-distance lorry driver helped to give him a little respite in between her shopping addiction, never knowing what he would be coming home to next.

Malcolm was less of a Yorkie bar and more of a full-fat family-size man. But as long as they were happy, who was I to judge?

I watched her take off a hairy cerise-knitted hat, stroke it, and gently place it on the table in front of her. A bit like rubbing your head and patting your stomach at the same time, she tried to adjust her hearing aids whilst flattening the static in her short, silver hair. Her fingers fumbled with the toggles on a technicolour dream coat. A sparkly chain took the weight of her red-rimmed glasses. Reminiscent of an expensive Christmas decoration, a rhinestone parrot took pride of place on her left lapel. It was like watching a Rod Hull and Emu sketch; at any second, Aunt Bren would be on the floor with her legs in the air with the parrot pecking her to death.

But her hips wouldn't cope with any of those carry-ons these days. She had already had her left one done and the last thing she needed was a fracture to the right. The only leg over that she got these days was sliding off her bath chair and into a goodnight sweetheart bubble bath. Her purple motor scooter was a necessary evil for covering more than a few steps. It was just a good job that the Potters Arms had installed a ramp and widened its doors. That was the least that they could do for her. After all, she had lined the pub's pockets in one way or another for many long years. Quite often she whirled in for a bit of gossip, just for old times' sake. But to be honest, this was one place where she felt closest to her Tony.

One day, she would get around to scattering his ashes, but at least he wasn't at the bottom of her wardrobe anymore. When she moved in with Max and Wayne, they insisted on finding a place for Tony on her dressing table. That new matching mahogany urn with 'Je taime' engraved on a brass nameplate was such a thoughtful gesture. Every night, before getting into her new posh bed that was adjusted with a flick of a switch, she placed a kiss on the top of Tony's box. A simple golden teardrop hung around her neck, carrying a bit of him with her until it was time to meet again.

But not even the best of the Infirmary's new mixologists could conjure a cocktail to get on top of her pain. But Bren had always been a cup-half-full kind of a girl and she wasn't going to let it get in the way of making the best of what she had. It was amazing what you can do with a good chemical peel and a touch of Botox these days. If it was good enough for Joan Collins, then it was certainly good enough for Aunt Bren. And just like Joan, I told her to keep her elbows covered. Like a sliced tree trunk, they never lied about a lady's true age.

I was just glad to have the opening slot at the LBGTQIA+ conference. Matt Ogston, founder of the Naz and Matt Foundation was speaking a little later in the day. Matt is a complete hero. In brief, the Naz and Matt Foundation was set up in 2014 following the tragic loss of Matt's fiancé, Naz, who took his life two days after his deeply religious family confronted him about his sexuality. Through his own experiences, Matt's mission is to never let religion come in the way of the unconditional love between parents and their children. And here I was, standing on the shoulders of giants with my own story to share. Taking a deep breath, I stepped out onto the stage and began:

"Hello everyone, and thank you for allowing me to chat with you all today. My name is Max. I know it will be hard for some of you to believe as you stare at my youthful appearance in disbelief, but I have been qualified as a registered nurse for over thirty years. Yes, you can cheer if you want to. Trust me, I have seen the good, the bad and the ugly of NHS leadership over this time. Sometimes, it makes me judder when I think about it. But for me, it's quite simple to get right; kind of inclusive, and compassionate, leadership is as crucial as breathing. One should not exist without the other.

"Some of you will know me as a senior clinical nurse. You are probably already yawning and expecting me to bore the pants off you with that today. Keep hold of your gussets, I'm going to do something very different. Today we are going to talk about love. Wayne, (my long-suffering husband) and I, use our adoption story to help and support others. This includes prospective adopters or people with children already placed with them. Whilst I am chatting today, I want to ask you to dig deep and consider if *you* are a thrower of starfish'. You may not be able to save thousands of them on the beach, but can you make a difference to every starfish that you throw back into the water? Before I start properly, I thought it was only right to ask my children what they think about having a 'Dad and a Daddy'. They wanted me to tell you that, 'We love having a Dad and a Daddy, it's really fun. We get treated properly. They have taught us what it is like to be loved and have kind people in our life. We love our Dad and Daddy more than anything else in the world.'

"So where did it all begin? A little over eight years ago now, we adopted two children from the care system to give them a loving forever home. It is their life story to hold, so please forgive me if I don't focus on the reasons why they came into care before they joined us. The most powerful thing that we have said to our children is that 'Dad and Daddy have adopted you because we love you and want you forever.' They know that we are not being paid to look after them. It is not our job. We have two fantastic children who are now growing up at a rate of knots. We really must stop planting them in compost every night. However, they wanted you to know that when they moved in with us, they were, 'Angry, confused and frustrated. It was a little bit scary because we changed homes, and everything changed around us. We didn't know what to do.'

"Our adoption journey started around ten years ago. It was triggered by my sister's breast cancer diagnosis. During her chemotherapy and radiotherapy treatment, we became part-time carers for her two young children. She simply wasn't strong enough to care for them. Through this experience, we were faced with trying to make sense of questions such as 'Is Mummy going to die, Uncle Max?' We also learnt that maybe we had some skills to support children. Life is strange, isn't it? Our family tragedy triggered our adoption journey. As they say, 'life is not about waiting for the storm to pass, it's all about learning to dance in the rain'.

"We were welcomed by the adoption service with open arms from start to finish. Our whole intense process took about twelve months to complete. It was an emotional roller-coaster and perhaps the hardest but the most worthwhile thing that we have ever done. Nearing the end of the adoption journey, we attended an adoption party. In brief, an adoption party, originally an American concept, is organised and run by adoption agencies. Prospective adopters are invited to play with looked after children who need a forever loving home. As you can imagine, this is a really difficult thing to do for everyone involved.

We knew all about our children's history before we went. However, this only made us want them more. We will never forget the first time that we saw them. I think the world stopped spinning for a brief moment. Both Wayne and I looked at each other and cried as everything that we had done as a couple over the years just seemed to be leading to this one moment. The first thing our children did was to jump on top of us and to snot in our faces. That has not changed, to be honest, over the years. They still do that now. When talking to our children about the adoption party, they wanted me to say, 'It was a bit confusing because we hadn't been told the truth about why we were there. We thought it was a birthday party. Our foster carer hadn't been honest with us. We had fun playing with Dad and Daddy though, but we didn't know who they were back then.'

"We have met some fantastic foster carers who do great jobs looking after children who are often vulnerable and traumatised. Unfortunately, our foster carer fell short of our expectations. During the adoption party, she made her feelings crystal clear. It just isn't morally or spiritually right for gay people to adopt. Only a mummy and daddy would do. Well, at least we knew where we stood with her. She even tried to control the social situation by funnelling our kids to play with heterosexual couples only. It was no surprise that she did her utmost to sabotage their planned transition from foster care to our home, either. She was lower than a snake's belly, using our children as pawns in her wicked game. Our social worker referred to her as a silent assassin. This experience was such a shame for everyone involved, but in particular our children.

"Our children go to fantastic schools. The teachers go above and beyond what is expected of them. The headteacher has been our knight in shining peroxide. Picture a cross between Bet Lynch and Marylyn Monroe. But it has not been an easy journey together. Yes, we are the first gay couple to have adopted within the local area. Our children are also the first to have a Dad and Daddy at school. So what, get over it. Sometimes people make mistakes by simply not thinking about what they are doing or saying. I have seen this both within my professional and personal life. But if something is wrong, it needs calling out and fixing. My youngest, burst into tears one night after school because they were forced to practice a Mother's Day assembly at school. They were made to sing 'you are my mummy, my only mummy' to the tune of 'you are my sunshine, my only sunshine'. Marching into my blonde nemesis's office, I spat my child's words at her, 'I am not upset because I haven't got a mummy. I am upset because all kinds of families should be celebrated and I want to make sure that my Dad and Daddy are included.'

"Wayne and I were also challenged by the head teacher on our ability to nurture. Apparently, children need strong female figures to do this properly. In an e-mail, she told us that men are not any good at this sort of thing. This led to many heated discussions around gender stereotyping.

"Healthcare professionals have been an education for our family. Even our local doctor's surgery, who are aware of our kid's history, got it dreadfully wrong in the early days. Again, with lots of support and education, there has been a change in practice. Staff no longer say things like 'Don't forget to tell your mummy about it when you get home'.

"So let us finish where we started when I asked you to dig deep. As you can see from listening to our story that Wayne and I are doing our best to be throwers of starfish. We are trying to make a difference in the lives of two children with our therapeutic, consistent and loving parenting.

"Now don't worry, I am not asking you to adopt a child or two unless you really want to do so. And if you do, then give me a shout and I will help. However, as professionals, I truly believe that we can *all* be 'throwers of starfish' in some way. All we need to do is to put the patient at the centre of what we do, listen and engage with our local community and ensure that we are all-inclusive leaders.

"In their own words, our children wanted to sum up our story with, 'We are proud to be adopted and we love our Dad and Daddy.'

"Thank you."

And with that, I stumbled from the stage with the warmth of the audience washing over me.

When I had regained control of my legs, Danni smiled and said,

"You did well up there Max, I'm so proud of you. But don't go mad with me, I just couldn't help myself. Those kids mean the world to me and if I want to spoil them, then I will."

"What have you bought then this time Danni? You have given them so much already."

And when I thought about it, it wasn't just our children that Danni had given so much to over the years. From out of a large netted rope bag, she produced two identical rainbow-coloured teddy bears. These deliciously soft toys beamed with excitement as she waved them at me.

"The kids will love them, Max. I couldn't resist them as I was walking past that 'make a toy workshop' at the shopping village the other day. I'm just glad that the kids weren't with me though. They would have been traumatised. No child needs to see how and where a bear gets its filling. Take a closer look, Max. Can you see what they are holding?"

"Why are they holding their own toy passports? They are so realistic though. I just think that their ID photo gives it away".

"Well, Bren and I have been plotting on the quiet. Sit down, I have got so much to tell you."

And just as I thought that my day couldn't get any better it did. Over lunch, this dastardly duo revealed their plans. Danni's parrot once again danced in glee as she told me what she had been up to behind the scenes. It was as if she was glued to a shopping channel summer sale, frantically filling her basket before they were 'sold out'. There was a method in her madness, though. Danni had picked up quite a bit about attachment theory.

"Well, it's like this. It's a lovely way of introducing your kids to the idea of a holiday abroad. Now, just hear me out before you start sucking on your teeth. I know that you are great at showing the children that not all change is bad. I have seen you do this over the years."

Danni and Bren had given so much thought to their master plan. I couldn't help but be impressed. They thought that the soft toys would be a starting point to introduce the idea of going on a family holiday. But they all wanted to tag along, too. Bren would be fine as long as she was dosed up on codeine for the journey. I smiled and imagined pushing this drug mule through the airport. Danni explained that a holiday could be a fun experience for our children. However, she knew that a lot of pre-teaching was needed beforehand. She suggested that we could break everything down into bitesize meaningful chunks. Such preparation could include 'talking' to the bears about their positive experiences of travel and looking at their passports. Other strategies may include reading bedtime books concerning air travel. A 'try before you buy' approach would be helpful. This experiential learning would include taking our children on field trips to the departing airport in advance. Our children would need reassurance that 'Dad and Daddy' would be with them every step of the way.

What could I say? She had thought of everything except for a few crucial points,

"Er, ok, I think. I'm sure Wayne will be up for it. But where are we going and how much will it cost?"

"Well, don't you worry about a thing? Your fairy godmother will come to the rescue on that one. What are pension pots for, anyway? After all, there are no pockets in shrouds. Wayne will know that from his mortuary days. I would like to take us to a complex of bungalows which are slap-bang in the middle of Playa Del Ingles. It's in Gran Canaria. That way, 'hop along Bren' over here won't have far to go."

God, that woman never failed to surprise me. After all of these years, she was still able to bowl me over with her kindness. And then she dropped the bombshell.

"Did you know that Adam has opened up another drag bar over there in the Yumbo Centre? Here, let me show you his website on my phone."

And there she stood in a long blonde curly wig, fringed cowgirl dress and probably one of the biggest breastplates that I had ever seen. Miss Nancy Eclair still looked as good as she did all of those years ago. There was a troop of younger drag queens on either side of her in the picture. Marylyn, Shirley, Marlena, Cher, Whitney, Bette, Beyonce and Celine smiled at us. It was amazing how Nancy had managed to get such torch singers all booked into one place. Especially as some of the lineup were dead. That must have taken some doing.

After a hard day of playing in the pool with water guns, our children had gone out like a light. They were tucked up together in bed, each holding their rainbow-coloured Teddy as they slept. Danni was right. The bears had worked like a treat. I sat and watched them for a while as they gently snored. It was the only time that the kids were still. We were so lucky to have them. Gently creeping over, I placed a kiss on their forehead before it was Wayne's turn. Malc and Bren whispered goodbye to us as we gently closed the door behind us for a night on the town. Danni looked beautiful. She wore a pink tropical print maxi dress and a pair of red sparkly mules. She was carrying a matching clutch bag. These were some of her better purchases from the shopping channel's fashion hour. The sun had whitened the tips of her silver hair and had bronzed her complexion.

Wayne had scrubbed up well, too. If anything, his appearance had got even better with age. He looked so handsome wearing my favourite shade of blue linen shirt. The top couple of buttons were open to reveal a wisp of his downy brown chest hair. A cream pair of cargo shorts framed his firm buttocks. His long, muscular legs led down to a pair of brown leather gladiator sandals. God, I had done so well for myself. Now more than ever, I really did understand the words to *Song on the Sand*, as we paraded along the promenade together. *Though the time tumbles by, there is one thing that I am forever certain of, I hear la da da da da da da da da da da da da, And I'm young and in love.* And I certainly was.

It was like turning back time. People of all shapes, colours and sizes were queuing around the block to get a glimpse of the one and only 'Miss Nancy Éclair'. She was as statuesque and slender as the first time that I had met her. When she spotted us through the weight of those beautiful beaded lashes, she pranced over and hugged us. Learning to mince in three-inch heals was an art form in itself. She shimmered over us in Hooker's green iridescence before saying,

"Come here, let Nancy crinkle you all. Mwah, Mwah. Now look, you have got my cherry lipstick on your cheeks. Oh my life, I have missed you all so much. It's been far too long. And look at you Danni, have you been on the formaldehyde again? Aren't you the love child of Marilyn Monroe and Marlon Brando? You don't age. Every time I see you, you look younger. And how could Nancy ignore you two handsome brutes? Please forgive Nancy. I almost popped out of my meaty tuck when I spotted you two studs. If it isn't my very own George Clooney and Elvis Presley. You smell good enough to eat. Mmmm, can I come back for seconds? And Nancy has heard that you are Dad and Daddy now. Condragulations. I'm green with envy. But you do know that I have a family of my own all over the world, don't you? They are my Nancy boys, girls or any label they choose or not, as the case may be. But they call me Mama Nance. Can I be Mama Nance to your children too? Adam will be along first thing in the morning to meet them. Apologies in advance. He is very quiet and may bore the tits off you all. But he loves kids, though."

Nancy had themed her bar loosely upon *The Wizard of Oz*. She escorted us along a yellow brick road and to a VIP booth upon the staged seating, smiling and posing for selfies with her adoring fans on the way through her club. She truly had found her feet in those three-inch heels. Leaning into us, she giggled and said,

"Now, please excuse Nancy. Make yourselves at home. Nancy needs to go and get ready for the show. Max has sat for many an hour and watched my transformation. Gosh, I miss those days. If only just once I could...."

And then she stopped in midsentence, dabbed the tears from the corner of her beaded lashes and slapped on her smile again. We slipped into a horseshoe emerald banquette. Instead of slippers, sparkly ruby drapes encased this prime spot. At any given moment, I thought that Glenda would drift over, appear from her pink bubble and take our drinks order. Instead of glasses, our green smoking witch's tit was served in upturned tin man hats. Such attention to detail had been the hallmark of Nancy's recipe for success. She was now a brand and a global franchise. Whilst there was a chain of similar bars all over the world, there was only the one Miss Nancy Éclair. On hearing that we were coming over on holiday, she had dropped her New York engagements and flown in on her broomstick to meet us.

The stage was set as the emerald city. A laser display tricked the mind into believing that it was all real. I imagine that after a couple more 'witch's tits, it probably would be. My experienced pallet tasted bourbon and crème de menthe, but God knows what else was in it. Either way, it was hitting the right spot. The bar was themed and positioned like a cabin just dropped from the sky. Everything was on the wonk, even the beer pumps. The bar staff were dressed as the characters from the movie. A gaggle of butch Dorothy's in gingham dresses and ruby slippers flirted shamelessly with the patrons for tips as they brought the drinks to the tables. And it worked. They were being fed like slot machines with notes into various parts of their bodies. The bigger the bill, the bigger the thrill.

A green glow darkened the auditorium. Munchkins in the cheap seats sizzled in anticipation for the show to start. A few lines of Harvey Fierstein's *I am What I Am* burst out from the surround sound system. The speakers in our seats vibrated to give us a truly immersive experience. I just managed to grab hold of Wayne's drink before it danced off the table. A spotlight flickered and then fixed upon a slit in the doors to the emerald city. A solitary silhouette stood with one hand on her hip and the other reaching for the sky. And then, in a split second, Miss Nancy Éclair appeared from behind the embossed doors. The audience shrieked in delight. They had not seen her perform this routine in years. It was an honour and a privilege that such drag queen royalty would resurrect this vintage number for her adoring fans. And there she stood, pregnant in a long blond wig, a Princess Kate-inspired wedding dress and three-inch silver heals. She was carrying a netted bag of foam house bricks. And then the opening bars of Yvonne Fair's *It Should Have Been Me* bellowed out as Nancy launched into action. It wasn't long before she was hitting me with those bricks all over again.

Oh my god, these witch's tits were sharp as they were strong. I stood up, burped, laughed and apologised to Wayne and Danni. It was a good job that they were family. Well, it had been a long time since we had let our hair down. The kids were safely tucked up in bed, after all. Another round of drinks magically appeared from a six-foot Dorothy who looked a little like Harry Styles on his Harryween Tour. I bet that this waiter had no difficulty getting tips. The room swayed in the emerald haze as we watched the rest of the world-class drag show. *The stars of yesteryear were alive and well* at Nancy's Cabaret Bar. And then I shuddered and grabbed hold of Wayne and Danni. Was it the witches' tit, too much sun, or what I wanted to see? God only knows. I was pinned to the spot and stared out onto the stage.

Nancy Éclair appeared from stage left, wearing a short, shimmering white dress that was fringed in tassels. As she bobbed onto the stage, her breastplate manically danced in rhythm to the country twangs. She was festoon in an even bigger blonde wig than in her opening number. It must have weighed an absolute tonne on her poor neck. Whilst tapping her thigh to the beat of the melody, she started to lip-sync to the first line of the song, *Baby, when I met you there was peace unknown, I set out to get you with a fine tooth comb, I was soft inside, there was something going on.* With the most accurate impression of Dolly that I have ever heard, she drooled,

"Please welcome to the stage Mr Kenny Rogers."

And then my heart missed a beat. Everything else faded away. I couldn't hear the rapture of the crowds or see anything but the centre of the stage. *You do something to me that I can't explain. Hold me closer and I feel no pain. Every beat of my heart, we've got something going on.* Nancy towered over her beau, as he filled the room with a golden aura, shaking a silver tambourine in perfect time to the song. He looked at me in the eyes. *Tender love is blind, It requires dedication, All this love we feel needs no conversation.* And he was right, he didn't need to speak. Love radiated from under his short blonde spiky quiff, tight white shirt and strategically placed pair of denim shorts. My translucent tin soldier in all of his clumsy glory was standing directly in front of me. Before fading into the night air he whispered in my ear, *Islands in the stream, That is what we are, no one in between, how can we be wrong?*

About the Author

Max Austin has many passions in his life; his husband, his two children, his writing and his work as a nurse. Oh, and not to forget the family dog of course! He lives with his husband, two children and dog in a rather busy but fun-filled household in Staffordshire, United Kingdom. He has worked as an authentic qualified nurse for over thirty years.

Through his writing and lived experiences, Max wants to give a voice to silenced and marginalised LBGTQIA+ groups. He is humbled that his own voice has found a home within Spectrum. Max has been a keynote speaker at LBGTQIA+ inclusion conferences. For Max, kind inclusiveness in health care and indeed our broader society is as vital as breathing.

When not working as a nurse or writing, he loves nothing more than spending time with his children and husband. Most weekends, they can be found covered in mud whilst being led through the park by their rather boisterous but friendly black Labrador!

Excellent LGBTQ+ fiction by unique, wonderful authors.

Thrillers

Mystery

Romance

Young Adult

& More

Join our mailing list here for news, offers and free books!

Visit our website for more Spectrum Books

www.spectrum-books.com

Or find us on Instagram

@spectrumbookpublisher

www.ingramcontent.com/pod-product-compliance
Lightning Source LLC
Chambersburg PA
CBHW010021130526
44590CB00047B/3756